RO
ME

Travel with Marco Polo Insider Tips

T0001356

MARCO POLO
TOP HIGHLIGHTS

COLOSSEUM ⭐ 1
The biggest arena in the ancient world, where gladiators once grappled with beasts.
📷 *Tip: try to capture the sun rising through the arches*

➤ p. 30

ROMAN FORUM ⭐ 2
Temples, triumphal arches and togas – the Forum was the centre of ancient political life.

➤ p. 32

PANTHEON ⭐ 3
Dazzling ancient dome, especially when the sun pours through the skylight.

➤ p. 48

SAN PIETRO (ST PETER'S) ⭐
A church with space for 60,000. St Peter's (photo) is the most visited place of worship in the world and the centre of the Catholic faith.
📷 *Tip: use your zoom to get a shot of the basilica's dome through the Knights of Malta's keyhole (Piazza Cavalieri di Malta)*

➤ p. 60

FONTANA DI TREVI (TREVI FOUNTAIN) ⭐ 5
You can't paddle in the fountain of *La Dolce Vita*; instead, people throw in their coins.

➤ p. 52

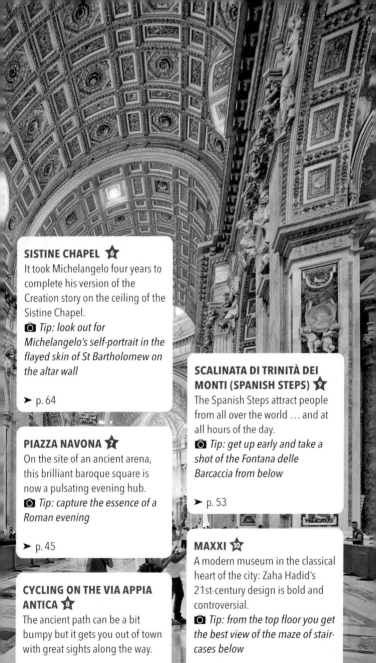

SISTINE CHAPEL ⭐
It took Michelangelo four years to complete his version of the Creation story on the ceiling of the Sistine Chapel.
📷 *Tip: look out for Michelangelo's self-portrait in the flayed skin of St Bartholomew on the altar wall*

➤ p. 64

PIAZZA NAVONA ⭐
On the site of an ancient arena, this brilliant baroque square is now a pulsating evening hub.
📷 *Tip: capture the essence of a Roman evening*

➤ p. 45

CYCLING ON THE VIA APPIA ANTICA ⭐
The ancient path can be a bit bumpy but it gets you out of town with great sights along the way.

➤ p. 141

SCALINATA DI TRINITÀ DEI MONTI (SPANISH STEPS) ⭐
The Spanish Steps attract people from all over the world … and at all hours of the day.
📷 *Tip: get up early and take a shot of the Fontana delle Barcaccia from below*

➤ p. 53

MAXXI ⭐
A modern museum in the classical heart of the city: Zaha Hadid's 21st-century design is bold and controversial.
📷 *Tip: from the top floor you get the best view of the maze of staircases below*

➤ p. 73

CONTENTS

Colosseum

⏱ Plan your visit	🍴 Eating/drinking	☂ Rainy day activities	
€–€€€ Price categories	🛍 Shopping	🐷 Budget activities	
(*) Premium rate phone number	🍸 Going out	🎭 Family activities	
		🚩 Classic experiences	

(*A2*) Refers to the removable pull-out map
(0) Located off the map

CONTENTS

BEST OF
ROME

Fontana di Trevi

BEST ☔

WHEN IT RAINS

ACTIVITIES TO BRIGHTEN YOUR DAY

TOURING THE CITY ON A TRAM

Board the no. 19 at Ottaviano-San Pietro. Its route takes in the Villa Borghese Park on the way to the Porta Maggiore, where you change on to the no. 3, which will trundle all the way to Trastevere. 1.50 euros for 100 minutes out of the rain.

MAXXIMUM CONTRAST

Rome's ultra-modern museum of contemporary art and its daring architectural angles – designed by Zaha Hadid – will make you rethink space and time (photo).
➤ p. 73

SCULPTURAL CAPPUCCINO

If it's drizzling, the *Atelier Canova Tadolini* in Via Babuini, once the studio of the sculptor Antonio Canova, is a charming place to sip a *caffè*.
➤ p. 82

FOR CHOCOHOLICS

The trendy loft of the old *Said-Antica Fabbrica del Cioccolato* is where people come in all weathers to drink a delicious cup of hot chocolate and buy exquisite pralines.
➤ p. 84

GALLERIA ALBERTO SORDI

After decades of dilapidation, this Belle Époque beauty has been transformed into a shopping arcade with exclusive boutiques and beautiful cafés that can compete with the best in Milan.
➤ p. 95

DESCEND INTO THE CATACOMBS

Explore miles of subterranean passages that were hewn out of the tufa stone over 2,000 years ago. The *catacombs* will keep you out of the rain while you learn about the early history of Rome.
➤ p. 142

BEST 🐷
ON A BUDGET

FOR SMALLER WALLETS

SAVE WITH THE ROMA PASS
The Roma Pass 48/72 hours costs 32/52 euros and includes travel on trams, metro and buses as well as admission to one/two museums (not those in the Vatican) and discounts at others. You can buy it at information centres, ATAC offices and major transport hubs *(romapass.it)*.

VIEW OF THE ROMAN FORUM
If you just want to catch a glimpse of the *Foro Romano* and avoid paying the admission, there is a great view from the steps to the left of the *Campidoglio*.
➤ p. 37

SISTINE CHAPEL FOR FREE
To see the world's largest art collection, Raphael's Stanze and the Sistine Chapel without paying a penny, there is free admission to the *Musei Vaticani*

on the last Sunday of the month. However, this is not a secret among other tourists …
➤ p. 62

CLASSICAL MUSIC IN CHURCHES
The view of the baroque dome of *Sant'Ignazio* is a *trompe l'oeil* (a painted illusion). By contrast the sound of the choirs that you can enjoy inside is very real – and the seats at the back cost nothing (photo).
➤ p. 116

TAKE THE TRAIN TO THE MEDITERRANEAN
The almost 30km train trip to the beach resort of *Lido di Ostia* costs only 1.50 euros. Lovers of archaeology take the same train and get off one stop earlier at *Ostia Antica*.
➤ p. 145

BEST WITH CHILDREN

FUN FOR YOUNG & OLD

HOWL WITH THE WOLVES

According to legend, Rome's founders, Romulus and Remus, were raised by a wolf. So, it is no surprise that wolves are the stars of the show in the *Bioparc*. There are also 200 other species, including giraffes and flamingos. *Piazzale del Giardino Zoologico 1 | bioparco.it*

TEATRO SAN CARLINO

On the covered Pincio terrace in the park of Villa Borghese, the San Carlino puppet theatre stages modern puppet musicals and Commedia dell'Arte performances. *Tickets: sancarlino.it | Viale dei Bambini/Ecke Viale Valadier*

OFF TO THE PARK

At Villa Borghese, Rome's second park, you can hire bikes and rickshaws *(Porta Pinciana from 5 euros/hr)*, take a paddle on the *laghetto (3 euros/20 mins)* or go walking or jogging. There are plenty of spots to have a picnic or just hang out.

➤ p. 57

STATUE PARLANTI

These weathered figures were the internet of their day, three centuries ago. At night people would secretly hang letters around their necks to express disgust at their government. Today's Romans still hang furious letters of complaint on the *Pasquino* statue behind the Piazza Navona.

➤ p. 133

JOIN ASTERIX IN THE FORUM

Follow in the footsteps of Asterix on a walk through ancient Rome. The guides from *Walks Inside Rome (walksinsiderome.com)* know how to capture and keep kids' attention.

➤ p. 155

BEST ⚑

CLASSIC EXPERIENCES

ONLY IN ROME

DRINKING FOUNTAINS

Eleven aqueducts kept ancient Rome well supplied with water, and free drinking water still bubbles from numerous little fountains in the *Centro Storico*. Do as the Romans do: close your hand over the spring and let the water spurt into your mouth from the upper hole.

THE MOUTH OF TRUTH

When Romans fall in love, they visit the ancient lie detector known as the *Bocca della Verità*. The human-sized marble face in the atrium of Santa Maria in Cosmedin has never actually bitten off the hand of a cynical young lover – at least, not yet!

➤ p. 40

CAMPO DE' FIORI: FLOWER MARKET AND VANITY FAIR

The city's most popular vegetable market in the mornings, *Campo de' Fiori* attracts a fashionable crowd round the clock. It's a place to see and be seen.

➤ p. 44

STEP UP, SIT DOWN

Even if you've seen a thousand photos of these famous curving steps, the *Scalinata di Trinità dei Monti* (Spanish Steps) remains one of the best places to sit and relax. People come here to flirt, laugh, take photos and daydream.

➤ p. 53

WHERE POLITICIANS GET THEIR ICE CREAM

Gelateria Giolitti is a local institution. The prices are steep and the service often abrupt, but Italian politicians head down from the nearby parliament to sample the 40 flavours of ice cream available here (photo).

➤ p. 83

11

GET TO KNOW ROME

Via Daniele Manin

DISCOVER ROME

The Spanish Steps remain a popular meeting point for both Romans and tourists

Climb the steps from the dark, somewhat grungy Metro B underpass, barge through the turnstile and, suddenly, as you emerge into bright daylight, there, right ahead of you, is the compact, four-storey wall of the Colosseum, so close you can almost touch it. This ancient amphitheatre, where thousands of gladiators and wild animals were slaughtered with an imperial thumb gesture, will send a shiver down your spine.

FROM THE FORUM TO THE HIP AREA OF MONTI

From the Colosseum, head across the wide Via dei Fori Imperiali to Piazza Venezia. No matter how you are getting around, you cannot escape history in Rome. Here you are following in the footsteps of Caesar and Cicero who once

21 April 753 BCE
Romulus slays Remus and founds Rome

510 BCE
The Roman Republic begins

27 BCE-284 CE
The Imperial era

64 CE
Rome burns, so Emperor Nero crucifies Christians

313 CE
Emperor Constantine permits Christian worship

1471
Pope Sixtus IV founds the Capitoline Museums

1527
The Sack of Rome: 24,000 German mercenaries pillage

walked this route to the Senate in the Roman Forum. On summer evenings, the ruins of ancient Rome's government buildings are magically lit up; you may be able to hear the musical strains of a rock concert floating on the breeze from Circus Maximus, where brutal chariot races were once held (as reimagined in the classic 1959 film *Ben Hur*). Today, large stretches of the *via* are pedestrianised and, in the evenings, Romans love to stroll peacefully past the historic sites, before diving into the backstreets of the hip party area, Monti, which is situated behind the pillars of the Forum of Augustus. They might eat a slice of crispy pizza as they walk, or relax in a *green bar* such as Aromaticus with its vegan snacks, or sample *gelato al limone* at one of the excellent ice cream shops. Everything is close to hand in Rome – the sublime and the trivial, beauty and tat, 3,000 years of proud history, ancient marble occasionally interrupted by the odour of rubbish left on a street corner.

AROUND THE *PIAZZE*

The rugged Roman cobblestones are not suitable for high heels or towering wedges. Nonetheless, with the right sandals or walking shoes, it's worth exploring Rome on foot. To properly understand *"La Grande Bellezza"*, Rome's wonderfully decadent beauty, you need to hang out in one of the *piazze*, the city's open-air living rooms. The *piazze* show off the vibrance of Roman life with their markets, funfairs, cafés, bars and newsstands. They are a space to flirt and for Italians to showcase their impeccable taste and inimitable ultra-cool elegance.

Rome under the orders of Emperor Charles V

1871
Rome becomes the capital of the newly unified Italy

1922-43
Fascist dictatorship under Benito Mussolini

1970-89
"Years of Lead" – acts of terror by the extreme right and left

2000
Pope John Paul II declares a Holy Year

2013
Pope Francis elected

2019
Rome decides on a series of drastic measures to protect its ancient heritage

PAPAL ATMOSPHERE ON ST PETER'S SQUARE

Find the piazza that best suits you. The largest, grandest and most photographed piazza is, of course, St Peter's Square – where Pope Francis himself is one of the most popular sights in the Vatican. When the Argentinian pontiff appears on the balcony at Easter and Christmas for his festive blessings – the *urbi et orbi* ("to the city and to the world") – or when he drives around in the popemobile after a general audience, the atmosphere is uplifting – even hardened atheists will find themselves moved. For the Holy Year of 2016, 20 million pilgrims passed through the Holy Door, which is only opened every 25 years and is otherwise bricked up.

MINI SEA BATTLES IN THE PIAZZA NAVONA

Piazza Navona, now buzzing with elegant street cafés, was originally a papal gift. It is a great piece of fun and colourful architecture that can awaken a range of emotions as you walk

through it. Pope Innocent X did not just gift his beloved sister-in-law Olimpia the Palazzo Pamphilj (today's Brazilian Embassy), but also the entire Piazza Navona. It was built on the site of an ancient Roman arena and, in the 17th century, patrician aristocrats and church dignitaries revived the contests, cheering on the games from their palace windows. Where today you sip coffee, bullfights once raged and horse riders raced round the circuit, as in the Palio in Sienna; the piazza was even flooded with water for naval battles with miniature ships. Take time to admire the piazza's magnificent babbling fountain. Today, in the evenings, this area is transformed into a stage for buskers, portrait artists, tarot card readers and gold-painted mime artists who stand motionless like a statue with a stunning backdrop.

The great rotunda of the Pantheon is classical architecture at its finest

PANINI, PIAZZA, PANTHEON

Every evening, Rome's beautiful people, including stars and politicians, meet up by the Piazza della Rotonda for an *aperitivo*, before heading to a fancy restaurant. The *ragazzi* from the suburbs prefer to buy *tramezzini* and *panini* in the Via del Seminario and sit in front of Rome's oldest temple, the Pantheon. According to the inscription, it was built by Consul Agrippa in the days of Emperor Augustus. In fact, the monument with the dome, which graces the space in front, was erected 100 years later. But what difference do a few years here or there make to a 2,000-year-old beauty?

A SUNDOWNER ON THE CAMPO DE' FIORI

At sunset, when the Campo de' Fiori, Rome's colourful old fruit and vegetable market, has been cleared away, orange-coloured aperitifs fill the glasses as people meet to enjoy a Campari or Aperol Spritz – a custom which has the

Milan-based spirits company Cinzano (part of the Campari Group) rubbing its hands with glee. There are also great places to eat and enjoy the nightlife in the warren of surrounding streets, as well as in the *trattorie* of Rome's biggest village, Trastevere, on the other side of the Tiber. Although it has lost some of its raw charm, thanks to its gentrification, you can still find plenty of romantic spots, with babbling fountains, tabby cats dozing on doorsteps and some of the older inhabitants sitting in front of their houses and chatting into the long summer nights. Otherwise, the former worker's quarter is buzzing with young entrepreneurs who have renovated their miniature apartments but still lead a distinctly Roman lifestyle. Every morning they buy a newspaper from the newsstand, drink their espresso at the local *barista* and go shopping at the small *alimentari* or at the local food market on Piazza S. Cosimato.

WHERE DO THE CLERGY HANG OUT?
Just behind the Pantheon on the Via Santa Chiara, in-between the ivy-covered Piazza dei Caprettari and the Piazza di Minerva, a small elephant created by the baroque sculptor Bernini bears the weight of an excessively heavy obelisk. This is where the clergy have a boutique with everything a religious heart could desire – from purple-coloured bishop's robes to discreet grey underwear for nuns. "Over 200 years at your service" is the motto of Annibale Gammarelli, tailor to the Vatican. And yes, Pope Francis does have his cassocks made here.

MODERN ARCHITECTURE VS THE ANCIENT CITY
In a place defined by tradition, modernity can have a hard time fitting in. The MAXXI, Zaha Hadid's revolutionary Museum of Arts of the 21st Century, floats like a fluffy cloud over erstwhile barracks in the Flaminio district; Renzo Piano's futuristic Parco della Musica auditorium, which wasn't taken seriously at first, now attracts music lovers from around the world; and Romans have even come to accept the controversial glass and steel canopy designed by American architect Richard Meier to protect the altar of peace commissioned by Emperor Augustus. But that doesn't necessarily mean the locals have wholeheartedly endorsed any of these.

A SCRUM AT THE TREVI FOUNTAIN
One small, inconspicuous and overcrowded piazza in Rome inspires deep affection: the Piazza di Trevi, where the Fontana di Trevi, Italy's most famous fountain, gushes its water out into a broad, flat basin. From dawn until late at night people flock to the spray from the baroque spout. Is this because of the lasting attraction of the film, *La Dolce Vita*, when Marcello Mastroianni and Anita Ekberg jump into the babbling fountain on a cold night in February? Or is it the custom of throwing a coin into the fountain to ensure a safe return to the Eternal City? There is only one way to find out!

AT A GLANCE

2,873,000
population

Vatican: 793 (incl. 52 women)
Glasgow: 1,673,332

21 APRIL

Celebrated as
Rome's birthday
since 753 BCE

59.4km
Metro tunnel length

Catacombs: more than 150km
London tube: more than 400km

1,285km²
Area

Vatican: 0.44km²
London: 1,572km²

**TALLEST BUILDING:
ST PETER'S BASILICA**

136.57m

537 steps to the top

WARMEST MONTH

JULY
28.6°C

**BUSIEST
MONTHS**

MAY &
OCTOBER

CATS: AROUND 300,000

There is a Roman decree which says cats should stay living where
they were born

1.4 million
euros
end up in the Trevi Fountain each year

UNESCO WORLD HERITAGE SITE
Rome's historical centre
has around 25,000 sites

**50,000 SPECTATORS
FITTED IN THE COLOSSEUM
IN ANCIENT TIMES**

UNDERSTAND ROME

CIAO, BAMBINI

Where have all the children gone, giggling and screaming in backyards, and once as much a part of life in Rome as Vespa scooters, fountains and *gelato al limone*? Italy is regarded as a child-friendly country, but it has one of the lowest birth rates in the world, and Rome – with a mere 1.1 births per woman of child-bearing age – scores particularly badly. The clergy is aware of this. "Romans, be fruitful and multiply. Have more children!", pled Cardinal Camillo Ruini some years ago. The retort from a Green politician was that the cardinal was like a blind man speaking about colours. However, Don Camillo did have eyes to see, and it was obvious that in his prominent diocese there were more cats than kids playing in the back yards, and that the lines of washing across alleyways were no longer hung with children's clothes.

Even though the *mamma* with five *bambini* at home remains a role model in Italian society, in practice many young couples are reluctant to have more than one child. The mundane reason for this is a striking lack of support. Financial benefits and parental leave are a pipe dream in Italy. The same applies to nursery schools, organised sport and playgrounds for children. Only five per cent of under three-year-olds get a place in a crèche or nursery. And the *nonna*, the grandmother who once lovingly gathered all the *bambini* to her skirts, now goes out to work herself and has to cope with all the challenges of modern life.

POP(E)STAR

A different kind of shepherd: a metal crucifix around his neck, scruffy black shoes and a white skull cap on his wind-blown hair, Francis is a pope of hearts and minds. Believers flock to St Peter's Square and love how he spontaneously embraces the old and sick, or even offers to take an unknown priest or two 11-year-old school children on a tour in his open-top popemobile. Each year on his birthday, Argentinians dance a tango in St Peter's Square in honour of their *papa*.

Following the surprising resignation of Pope Benedict XVI, the Argentinian Jorge María Bergoglio was elected to the papacy on March 13, 2013. This former Archbishop of Buenos Aires has since caused quite a stir in the Catholic Church. Following in similar footsteps to St Francis of Assisi, he calls for a "church of mercy", and a "poor Church for the poor". This "world priest", now over 80 years old, takes the words mercy and charity seriously, and once spontaneously visited African refugees who had landed on the island of Lampedusa.

In his first year, Francis tackled head on the issues of corruption and money laundering within the Vatican Bank and asked victims of clerical sex abuse for forgiveness. As the first Jesuit and South American to take the Chair of

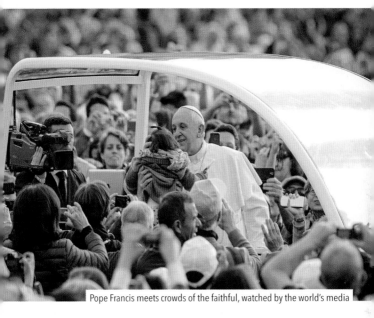

Pope Francis meets crowds of the faithful, watched by the world's media

St Peter, his views on contemporary issues such as contraception, divorce and celibacy are less defined and it remains to be seen whether he can bridge the deep divide between the Holy See and modern-day Christians. His views on abortion, which he has compared to contract killing, for example, have caused consternation among some. And there were protests over his remarks to journalists that much could be done "through psychiatry" if homosexuality were spotted at an early enough age (the remark was later deleted from the official record).

Even some of his fans are beginning to wonder if the breath of fresh air that accompanied him on his arrival at the Vatican is beginning to go stale. There is every chance that Francis's star could begin to fade.

LUXURY WASTE

Every Italian knows the luxury fur brand of Fendi. Ilaria Venturini Fendi, the granddaughter of the founders of this famous fashion house, has turned heads by moving into organic farming and recycled fashion. Her grandmother Adele founded a fur and leather shop in Rome in 1918 and Adele's five daughters transformed the business into a global brand. In the 1990s, *alta moda* suffered a series of crises with the growth of mass production and counterfeit products. Ilaria, who had by then joined the family company, suffered personally when militant animal rights activists sprayed the fashion company's fur coats red and also destroyed entire collections made from valuable animal products. She left the company in

2006 and founded her own recycling brand *Carmina Campus* (Latin for "odes to the field"). The name is no coincidence as Ilaria is also a farmer producing her own organic Pecorino cheese with milk from "happy sheep" on her estate outside Rome. Many of

UN women's organization in Kenya. Even former First Lady Michelle Obama bought one of the purple handbags with the eco statement "Water is Life", which are available from the *Re(f)use* boutique, located directly opposite the Fendi luxury temple on the Largo Goldoni *(carmina campus.com, fendi.com)*.

WEDDINGS ON CAPITOL HILL

Roman bridal couples used to say, "I do" in one of Rome's many churches. Today, most prefer a *matrimonio civile*, especially since Rome's most popular Registry Office is in the Palazzo Senatorio on the Capitol, one of the most magical venues in the world. Celebs and politicians also get married here (often for the second or third time). In 2016, the Mayor Virginia Raggi celebrated the first same-sex wedding between the Turkish film director Ferzan Özpetek and his Italian partner, after the Italian parliament approved same-sex civil weddings.

It's a wonderful moment for photographers and onlookers when happy newly-weds steal a kiss under the raised hand of Roman Emperor Marcus Aurelius (although the original statue is next door in the Musei Capitolini).

Two faces of the Fendi brand: *alta moda* and recycled art ∎

INSIDER TIP
Upcycling
à la Fendi

the cool green handbags made from old safari tents, mosquito nets, umbrellas and rubbish bags, or jewellery accessories created from recycled coke cans and sheet metal are manufactured by a

FONTANA DI EURO

Finance ministers around the world dream of a fountain like this, one that flows even in times of crisis: the Trevi Fountain. Every year, volunteers with the Catholic humanitarian charity Caritas fish 35,000kg of coins (often more than 1.4 million euros) out of

Rome's most beloved baroque fountain. Chances are that these sums will grow as the city of Rome has made it illegal for ordinary people to fish money out of the fountain. The cash can only be used for humanitarian purposes and not to fill holes in the tax budget. A large amount of it goes to Caritas and to a socially active humanist community of San Egidio in Trastevere.

FRESHLY SPONSORED

Advertising posters for pasta above the Spanish Steps or billboards for mobile phones on the scaffolding propping up the crumbling palazzi: Romans and tourists feel oppressed by the explosion of advertising on city monuments. But cultural sponsoring is on trend as the city of Rome is so short of cash. The fashion house Fendi, which recently donated 1.7 million euros for the restoration of the Fontana di Trevi, did not insist on large billboards around the fountain. Instead, the fashion empire staged its latest show at the venue: Fendi models ran about like modern-day nymphs on a glass catwalk above the sparkling fountain. Fortunately, there are also discreet sponsors who don't want much fanfare. Tod's, the huge shoe company, gave 25 million euros to renovate the tired Colosseum. They did not even insist on the legionaries who pose for photos with tourists outside the building swapping their cheap plastic sandals for a pair of Tod's.

The luxury jeweller Bulgari gave 1.5 million euros to clean the Spanish Steps of leftover pizza, chewing gum

TRUE OR FALSE?

MAMMA MIA

We have all seen the films: an Italian mother, with a huge brood of kids, cooking spaghetti in a pinny and yet still managing to look like Sophia Loren, despite the rings under her eyes. But, in fact, Rome, like most of the Western world, has very low birth rates. Having said that, even in modern times Italians tend to remain dependent on their *Mamma* (with a capital "M") and generally stay very close to the family.

PAVAROTTI & THE PARTISANS

Italians love to sing. Every taxi driver is a mini-Pavarotti, and family parties are nearly always serenaded with the hits of aging rockstar Gianna Nannini. Silvio Berlusconi, the former Prime Minister, liked to entertain his fellow world leaders with Neapolitan songs. In 2018 *"Bella Ciao"*, a 19th-century political song written by partisans about resistance to invaders, became a surprise summer hit. It was a direct challenge to then Minister for the Interior, Matteo Salvini, and his extreme anti-immigration politics. To this day, when he turns up anywhere, his opponents sing *"Bella, ciao, ciao, ciao"*.

Obelisks: stone souvenirs from the classical era

back then anyone walking around the square here could be forcibly recruited into the Spanish army.

SOUVENIRS FROM THE NILE DELTA

Tourists come back from Venice with models of gondolas and from Paris with the Eiffel Tower. In the Caesars' days, however, one of the pencil-like, massive stone obelisks that the ancient Egyptians erected to honour their sun gods was the "in" souvenir for a general. Rome's most beautiful squares are home to twelve of them. The first was brought from Heliopolis by Augustus, and the last was looted from Axum in Ethiopia by Benito Mussolini in 1937 to add splendour to his residence, Villa Torlonia. However, after a lengthy campaign, it was returned to Ethiopia in 2004. A hunt for these status symbols doubles up as a tour of the best sights in the city: they stand in front of St Peter's, the parliament and the Pantheon, on Piazza Navona and Piazza del Popolo, in front of the Quirinal Palace, the church of Santa Maria Maggiore and the Baths of Diocletian, high above the Spanish Steps and hidden away in the park of Villa Celimontana.

FEATHERED FRIENDS

Apart from their name, the monk parakeets have nothing to do with the Catholic Church. However, these South American migrants have travelled a long way to find new preferred perches in the Vatican's gardens where their fellow South American, Pope Francis, likes to take a

and red wine. Since the steps were once Spanish territory, the Spanish government (thanks to this once being the site of the Spanish embassy to the Vatican) could perhaps have contributed a pound or two. After all,

stroll. No one knows exactly how they got all the way to Rome – it could have been under their own steam, or in the hold of a plane, or else they may have escaped from a cage in someone's house. What is certain is that these green-grey parrots seem to like the Roman climate and have begun to spread around other parks in the city.

In Caffarella Park on the Via Appia Antica there are parrots from all over the world – a veritable UN of them – thanks to the employees of a pet shop who released their leftover birds after their shop closed down. Reproduction has done the rest …

PAPAGALLI & PAPARAZZI

The dictionary will tell you that *papagallo* has three different meanings: a) parrot, b) pot for urinating, c) pestering admirer. In the 1960s, the last of these three gained something like VIP status in Rome, when every pretty blonde or blue-eyed girl wanted to find out for herself whether what the magazines wrote was really true: that passionate Latin lovers awaited them by the Spanish Steps, softly whispering *"Ciao bella"* and *"ti amo"* as they offered to show visiting beauties around one of the world's most seductive cities. Perhaps the *papagalli* deserve medals for their services to European unity: many a handsome *ragazzo* of those days is still attached to his blonde *amore*.

Papagalli and paparazzi – hunters of skirts and celebrities – actually have little in common, except that they are both products of film director Federico Fellini's imagination. In the film *La*

Monk parakeets can be found in the Vatican's gardens

Dolce Vita the journalist Marcello (Marcello Mastroianni at his best) and his photographer, a man named Paparazzo, get into all sorts of trouble on Via Veneto – usually on the receiving end of US movie star Lex Barker's fists. This gave birth to the term "paparazzo" for a tabloid photographer. To this day, the paparazzi remain hot on the trail of celebrity snaps.

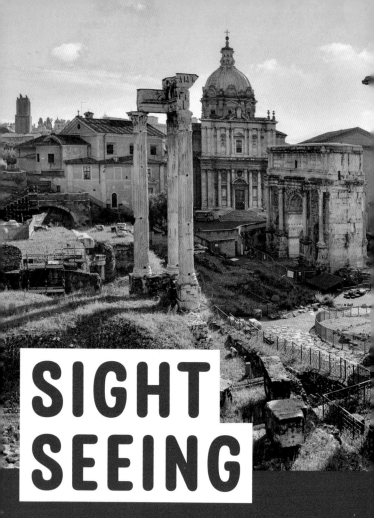

SIGHT SEEING

Rome is like a vast historical buffet where you have to pick out the best bits. Over its 3,000-year history, the city has acquired so many treasures that not even a computer could categorise them. There is nowhere else on earth where you will find so many wonders from so many different eras. Indeed, they are often stacked on top of one another like a wedding cake.

In 2000, when the futuristic Parco della Musica auditorium was being built, archaeologists discovered the remains of a 2,000-year-old villa, which is now ingeniously integrated into the building.

Forum Romanum

Simply ticking off the sights here can get exhausting so make sure to take lots of ice cream and cappuccino breaks. And take heart from the fact that some of the world's most famous writers and thinkers have been left speechless by Rome's churches, palaces, columns and ruins. Today there is the added challenge of long queues at the main sights; fortunately, most can be pre-booked online.

NEIGHBOURHOOD OVERVIEW

PRIMAVALLE

P.R.U. Pineto

Via Mattia Battistini

TRIONFALE

Circonvallazione Trionfale

PAPAL ROME p. 59

Vatican City – small but powerful

CIVITA VATICANA

Cappella Sistina ★ ◉
San Pietro (St Peter's) ★ ◉

MARCO POLO HIGHLIGHTS

★ **COLOSSEUM**
Bread and circuses in the ancient arena
➤ p. 30

★ **ROMAN FORUM**
Where Caesar and Cicero walked – the centre of power in the ancient world
➤ p. 32

★ **MUSEI CAPITOLINI**
Stars of antiquity: Venus, the Capitoline Wolf and the Dying Gaul ➤ p. 37

★ **CAMPIDOGLIO**
Michelangelo's trapezium-shaped Capitol square ➤ p. 37

★ **PIAZZA NAVONA**
Strut around the finest baroque stage ➤ p. 45

★ **PANTHEON**
A domed rotunda – one of the most iconic constructions in the ancient world ➤ p. 48

★ **FONTANA DI TREVI**
Rome's favourite fountain ➤ p. 52

★ **SCALINATA DI TRINITÀ DEI MONTI**
The place to meet: the Spanish Steps
➤ p. 53

★ **GALLERIA BORGHESE**
Bernini's sensual sculptures in a newly restored pleasure palace ➤ p. 57

★ **SAN PIETRO**
St Peter's Basilica: heart of the Roman Catholic world ➤ p. 60

★ **CAPELLA SISTINA**
Michelangelo's famous frescoes in the Vatican Museum ➤ p. 64

★ **CENTRALE MONTEMARTINI**
Ancient sculptures in a power station
➤ p. 71

★ **MAXXI**
Zaha Hadid's museum for contemporary art – a challenge to ancient Rome ➤ p. 73

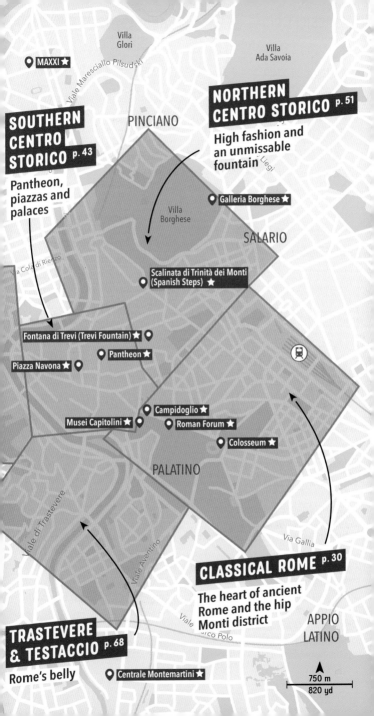

MAXXI ★

SOUTHERN CENTRO STORICO p. 43

Pantheon, piazzas and palaces

NORTHERN CENTRO STORICO p. 51

High fashion and an unmissable fountain

PINCIANO

Galleria Borghese ★

Villa Borghese

SALARIO

Scalinata di Trinità dei Monti (Spanish Steps) ★

Fontana di Trevi (Trevi Fountain) ★

Pantheon ★

Piazza Navona ★

Campidoglio ★

Musei Capitolini ★

Roman Forum ★

Colosseum ★

PALATINO

CLASSICAL ROME p. 30

The heart of ancient Rome and the hip Monti district

APPIO LATINO

TRASTEVERE & TESTACCIO p. 68

Rome's belly

Centrale Montemartini ★

750 m
820 yd

CLASSICAL ROME

From the Capitol to the Lateran: Rome's marble beginnings can be found here between the imperial forums, triumphal arches and the Colosseum. And in Santa Prassede is one of the finest golden mosaics of the Middle Ages.

In Monti, as this popular quarter is called, you can take a trip back in time, making lots of stops along the way. Close to the postmodern Stazione Termini, you will find the largest baths in the Roman Empire, the majestic Papal Basilica of Santa Maria Maggiore and Michelangelo's impressive *Moses*. Descend into the underground domains of San Clemente or climb up to the square on the Capitoline Hill. Monti was a red-light district in classical times and is rumoured to be where the lustful empress Messalina hung out. Back then it was called Suburra and it has retained some of the old underground charm to this day, with narrow streets, small houses, pretty shops, good trattorias and a red-light district straight out of Fellini's *Roma*.

Experience the charm of Roman traditions around the Piazza Santa Maria in Monti, the nightlife in the Via dei Serpenti or the Sunday street festival between the Colosseum and the Capitol, when the Via dei Fori Imperiali is closed to traffic. Hopefully the section from the Piazza Venezia to Via Cavour will remain open only to residents' vehicles – it has become a wonderful place to stroll around.

◘ COLOSSEUM ★

Stamping feet, the sound of drums and trumpets, and deafening cheers from the crowds when a gladiator fell wheezing to the ground. Metal glinted in the sunlight, while the dust was stirred up. The Emperor fanned himself with a handkerchief; the same piece of fabric that he used to preside over life and death. He was usually generous enough to leave the decision to his people: the Senators and salaried workers, the nobility and slaves who had the power to send the defeated gladiator to his death with the cry *"iugula"* ("kill him!"), or occasionally to show mercy and hiss *"missum"* ("release" or "send away"). Gladiators were usually professional fighters and highly trained men, yet their social rank was lower than that of slaves. The winner received a laurel wreath, money and gifts, such as the affection of a beautiful lady… and the certainty of getting killed in a future contest.

The gigantic arcades of the Colosseum were Emperor Vespasian's attempt, as successor to the cruel Nero, to enhance his popularity. He staged "bread and circuses" events, like modern statesmen host a World Cup or the Olympic Games. The project, initiated by Vespasian senior in 72 CE, was inaugurated by his son and successor, Titus, after just eight short but intensive years of building. Nowadays, major projects (such as Crossrail) require a similar timescale just for the planning phase. Technically the majestic Colosseum was a masterpiece. The arena had seating capacity of 50,000 spectators; the first three rows were reserved for the Roman aristocracy. Women, slaves and plebeians crowded into the top wooden stand below sun canopies. The sophisticated underground passages, trap doors, enclosures and lifts for wild animals are still visible today in the foundations of the building as the changing rooms and weapons stores for the gladiators. Safety guidelines were also extremely advanced: in the case of an emergency, such as a fire, the arena could be cleared in five minutes via 80 entrances and exits.

Today, the Colosseum is not only one of Rome's major attractions with

Gladiators once fought in the mighty Colosseum

The Roman Forum was the centre of political power in Ancient Rome

more than five million visitors a year, but it's also a proud memorial in opposition to the death penalty: since 1999 the monument has been bathed in green light every time a state decides to abolish the death penalty. If you don't manage to get there in the day, the romantic "Luna sul Colosseo" night tours are well worthwhile (8pm–midnight). *Daily 8.30am until 1 hr before dusk | admission 12 euros (also valid 2 days for Foro Romano and Palatine), online reservation highly recommended at coopculture.it | Piazza del Colosseo 1 | Metro B Colosseo | ⊙ 1 hr plus extra time to queue | ⊞ G10*

INSIDER TIP
Colosseum in the moonlight

▣ ROMAN FORUM ★

From their office in Palazzo Senatorio on the Capitol, the mayor of Rome has the best view of this marble-clad centre of Ancient Rome's political power. The Forum Romanum was originally conceived as a sanctuary for six Vestal Virgins, whose job it was to look after Rome's sacred fire. Later it evolved from a cattle market to a political arena from which not only Rome but the whole Roman Empire was ruled. This is where Cicero gave his famous speeches condemning Catilina and where old Cato spoke his *ceterum censeo*: "Carthage must be destroyed." In the end Rome needed three wars to knock out its rivals for hegemony in the Mediterranean.

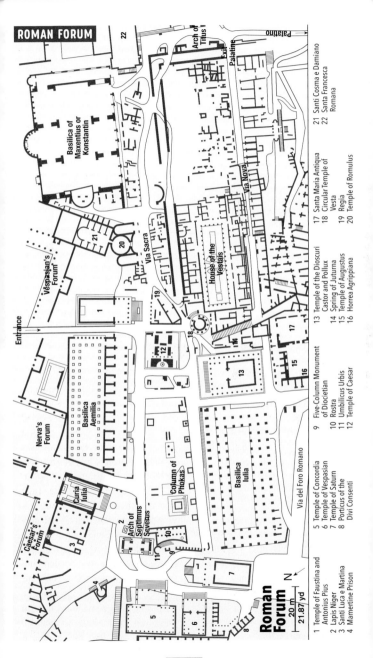

ROMAN FORUM

Roman Forum

N

20 m
21.87 yd

1 Temple of Faustina and
  Antonius Pius
2 Lapis Niger
3 Santi Luca e Martina
4 Mamertine Prison

5 Temple of Concordia
6 Temple of Vespasian
7 Temple of Saturn
8 Porticus of the
  Divi Consenti

9 Five-Column Monument
  of Diocletian
10 Rostra
11 Umbilicus Urbis
12 Temple of Caesar

13 Temple of the Dioscuri
   Castor and Pollux
14 Spring of Juturna
15 Temple of Augustus
16 Horrea Agrippiana

17 Santa Maria Antiqua
18 Circular Temple of
   Vesta
19 Regia
20 Temple of Romulus

21 Santi Cosma e Damiano
22 Santa Francesca
   Romana

Today you don't have to wear a toga to stroll between the columns and triumphal arches on warm summer evenings. These tours are called *"Roma sotto le stelle"* (Rome beneath the stars) *(in Italian and English | June–mid-Sept | dates from the tourist information pavilions and newspapers, e.g. La Repubblica)*.

Some things to look out for in the forum: from the entrance on Via dei Fori Imperiali you pass the *Basilica Aemilia*, *Tempio di Faustina*, *Tempio di Caesare* and *Arco di Augusto* and cross the *Via Sacra* to reach the *Rostra*, the stage for speakers; on the right is the *Lapis Niger*, the "Black Stone" above Romulus's grave, the *Curia* of the senate and the *Arco di Settimo Severo*; on the left the *Tempio di Saturno* and *Basilica Julia*, the court building that Caesar had built shortly before he was killed, the rectangular *Tempio di Castore e Polluce* and the circular *Tempio di Vesta*. Along the Via Sacra you pass the *House of the Vestals*, the *Tempio di Romolo* – which Maxentius built for a son who had died young – and the *Basilica di Massenzio*, altered by Constantine.

At the entrance near the *Arco di Tito*, a path leads up to Palatine Hill, where many rich Romans, among them Cicero and Catullus, possessed villas. You can walk back down to the forum through lovely 16th-century gardens, the *Orti Farnesiani*. *Daily 8.30am until 1 hr before dusk | admission 12 euros (includes Colosseo and Palatine, valid 2 days) | entrances: Largo Salara*

You only get this view of the Fori Imperiali from the roof of the Monumento Vittorio Emanuele II

CLASSICAL ROME

14 Terme di Diocleziano

13 Palazzo Massimo alle Terme

Roma Termini

11 Santa Maria Maggiore

6 Monumento Nazionale a Vittorio Emanuele II

Giardino del Quirinale

10 San Pietro in Vincoli

4 Campidoglio ★

3 Imperiali Fora

Parco del Colle Oppio

5 Musei Capitolini ★

Roman Forum ★ 2

1 Colosseum ★

9 San Clemente

8 Bocca della Verità

Piazza del Colosseo

500 m
547 yd

Parco del Celio

7 Circo Massimo

San Giovanni in Laterano 12

Vecchia (Via dei Fori Imperiali), Via di San Gregorio 30, Piazza Santa Maria Nova (Arco di Tito) | pre-booking tel. 06 39 96 77 00 | bus 85, 87, 117 | ☉ 2–3 hrs | ⌨ F9–10

3 IMPERIAL FORA

The Imperial Fora are most beautiful at night when the marble columns are illuminated and the places that defined Caesar and Augustus's reigns come back to life. Due to their resounding success, the historical light shows of "Viaggio nei Fori" are to be repeated (April–Oct daily from 8pm | with headsets available for English or Italian | info tel. 06 06 08 | viaggio neifori.it).

Foro di Augusto (F) (⌨ F9) (Piazzetta del Grillo 1 | bus 85, 87). The Forum of Augustus is the scene of one of Ancient

Rome's best detective stories. The boy Octavian, whose bronze bust looks slightly anxious, enjoyed a phenomenal rise to fame. After the murder of his great uncle Julius Caesar in 44 BCE, the 19-year-old successor prevailed against friend and foe and destroyed Caesar's assassins Brutus and Cassius. He was co-ruler for 13 years; later, as Emperor Augustus, he was the sole ruler for an astounding 43 years. Although he engaged in war, he was considered to be an emperor of peace due to his stability and continuity, not unlike Queen Elizabeth II. The forum is dominated by the temple of the vengeful Roman god of war, Mars. Augustus had more than 80 temples built or adorned. He is said to have found Rome a city of bricks and left it a city of marble.

There is a good view from Via dei Fori Imperiali.

Foro di Cesare (□ F9) (Via dei Fori Imperiali | bus 85, 87). Donald Trump may not have needed his presidential salary, but the wealth of Julius Caesar would have blown that of the ex-United States president out of the water. He had the entire government quarter built at his own expense. Still recognisable are the rows of shops, the remains of the Basilica Argentaria (which was used as a bank and exchange) and three surviving columns of the Temple of Venus. One day,

as the historian Suetonius relates, the consul received the senate seated on the base of the Temple of Venus. With this affront to piety – only gods were allowed to sit – Caesar claimed a status equal to Jupiter. Shortly afterwards he was murdered.

Foro di Traiano (□ F9) (Tue–Sun 9am until 1 hr before dusk | admission 11.50 euros, good view also from outside | Via IV Novembre 94 | bus 40, 64, 70, 170). The 38-m-high Trajan's Column, erected in 113 CE, is the centrepiece of the last and most magnificent of the imperial forums.

Reliefs on Trajan's Column depict the Emperor's war against the Dacians

It now gleams pearly white again after almost ten years of restoration. From below you can admire the 200-m sculptural frieze depicting Emperor Trajan's war against the Dacians.

4 CAMPIDOGLIO ★

This is still a magical place, even if today's Romans have mainly practical reasons for climbing the wide steps to the Capitol, the ancient seat of the gods. Frustrated and grumbling citizens go to the town hall in the Palazzo dei Senatori (straight ahead) to complain to the mayor about the inefficient administration or the constant rubbish collector strikes. Beaming happy couples, however, continue to the world's most beautiful registry office in the Palazzo dei Conservatori (right).

In 1536, Michelangelo laid out the trapezium-shaped square of the Capitol, where the Temples of Jupiter and Juno had once stood, flanked by the *Palazzo dei Senatori*, the *Palazzo dei Conservatori* and the *Palazzo Nuovo*. The pedestal from which the riding Emperor Marcus Aurelius greets passers-by with a raised hand today bears a copy of the original statue dating from the second century, which needed protection from pollution and was moved inside the *Musei Capitolini*.

➤ If you take the steps to the left of the Piazza del Campidoglio, you will get a wonderful view of the Roman Forum. On the way, pause to look at the small bronze statue of the Roman she-wolf, who was said to have raised the city's founders Romulus and Remus. If wolves have a fearsome reputation in other parts of the world, the Romans affectionately regard their fur-clad symbol, which is also the football mascot of AS Roma and a popular tattoo on their toned upper arms. *Piazza del Campidoglio | bus 30, 60, 62, 63, 64, 70, 81, 87, 117, 119, 160 | ⌕ F9*

5 MUSEI CAPITOLINI ★

The Vatican is not the only museum in Rome! The Capitoline Museums are smaller, easier to navigate and less crowded than the Papal competition. Ironically, they were sponsored by Pope Sixtus IV, who also commissioned the Sistine Chapel. His Holiness wanted to remove the naked statues from the Vatican and he left them as a legacy to the city in 1471 – thereby creating the world's first public museum.

INSIDER TIP *A prudish pope*

There are several exhibits which should not be missed. First, is Emperor Constantine's colossal, outstretched marble finger which in the ancient world was a powerful symbol of his dominance. Next, in the Sala della Lupa, the *Capitoline Wolf* is the symbol of Rome and the spiritual mother of all Romans as she suckled the city's founders Romulus and Remus. In the Sala delle Colombe, you can see the delicate Roman *Mosaic of the Doves*, where the birds of peace drink from a golden cup. It was discovered in the Villa Hadrian in Tivoli. If you want to see a well-built man with rippling muscles, then visit the

The Dying Gaul. The wounded warrior summons the last of his strength to sit upright; it's one of the most moving sculptures anywhere.

Too many men? Then admire the Goddess of Love: the *Capitoline Venus*, who is shown emerging naked from her bath. In 2016, during a visit from the Iranian President Rouhani, the statue was deemed unsuitable and was draped in a towel to protect her modesty.

However, the most spectacular exhibit is the original equestrian statue of Emperor Marcus Aurelius. Since 2005 it has been placed under a glass roof in the *Giardino Romano*, a courtyard of the Palazzo dei Conservatori. A copy stands on the Capitol square where people take photos of themselves under his raised hand. Treat yourself to a break in the cafeteria of the roof garden (accessible even if you are not visiting the museum) for a breathtaking view of the city. *Daily 9.30am–7.30pm | admission 11.50 euros; with Centrale Montemartini 12.50 euros; with exhibition 15 euros (valid 7 days) | Piazza del Campidoglio | bus 63, 95, 119, 160, 170, 638 | tram 8 | ⊙ 2 hrs | ▢ F9*

The original statue of Marcus Aurelius is a highlight of the Musei Capitolini

6 MONUMENTO NAZIONALE A VITTORIO EMANUELE II

Romans disrespectfully dub it the "typewriter", "wedding cake" or even the "false teeth". This snow-white marble pile on the Piazza Venezia certainly catches the eye. It is the National Monument to Victor Emmanuel II, the first king of Italy after unification in 1870. Now the monument houses the Museum of Italian Unification. It also allows access to its terraces. From the *Terrazza delle Quadrighe*, the highest platform with its decorative bronze horses, you get a superb view of the Forum Romanum and the whole city centre. *Daily 9.30am–5.30pm, in winter 9.30am–4.30pm | lift 7 euros | Piazza Venezia | entrance from S. Maria in Coeli | bus 30, 40, 85, 87, 119 | ▢ F9*

7 CIRCO MASSIMO

Chariot races were the Formula 1 of Ancient Rome. The glamour of the Circus Maximus resembled Monte Carlo during the Grand Prix. The emperor cheered on the death-defying chariot drivers who basked in the glory of fame and riches, just as Lewis Hamilton, Max Verstappen and others do today. Some empresses – such as Messalina – are rumoured to have invited the muscly victors to their bedchamber. Four horse-drawn chariots raced seven times anti-clockwise around the 350-m central barrier. Major crashes were commonplace and, as the side barriers were unpadded, injuries were often fatal for horses and their drivers. Horse races were already held here during the Etruscan period in the seventh century BCE; Caesar commissioned the expansion of the biggest racecourse (*maximus*, or largest) with marble step-seating for about 175,000 spectators; his successors created space for 250,000 racing fans. "Bread and circuses" *(panem et circenses)* were by then popular events for those seeking pleasure. There were plenty of betting booths where ordinary Romans could gamble away their sesterce, as well as smoke-filled bars and many brothels. Today, the Circus Maximus is a green, peaceful and tranquil place beneath the Palatine Hill. In summer, open-air concerts rekindle a magnificent atmosphere for many tens of thousands of fans. *Via del Circo Massimo | Metro B Circo Massimo | Bus 75 | tram 3 | ꛵ F10–11*

🟦 BOCCA DELLA VERITÀ ⚑

The "mouth of truth" is a strange marble face as tall as a man on the left of the atrium of Santa Maria in *Cosmedin*. The left eye seems to be shedding tears, and the mouth has been worn smooth as visitors place their hands into the monster's jaws. By tradition jealous married people send their partners there. If they don't tell the truth, this ancient lie detector is said to bite off the hand. After you remove your hand with a sigh of relief, briefly visit the 1,000-year-old gold mosaic inside the church that was created by the famous Cosmaten family of artists (cosmedin is Greek for ornament). *Daily 9.30am–6pm; winter 9.30am–5pm | Piazza Bocca della Verità 18 | bus 63, 30, 160, 170, 83 | ꛵ E10*

🟦 SAN CLEMENTE

This church is a bit like a tardis, taking you back through Rome's different historical periods until you reach Ancient Rome's sewage system, the *cloaca massima*, through which you can still hear water trickling today. The golden mosaics of the chancel arch and the apse of the medieval upper church are a gem. You then descend to the lower church (fourth century), dedicated to Clement, the fourth pope (88–97 CE), where fragments of frescoes depicting the life of the saint can still be discerned.

This columned basilica, which was destroyed by the Normans, lies in turn above a building used for the cult of Mithras, the Persian god of light, whom many Roman legionaries worshipped in bloody rituals associated with bulls. One level below that are the remains of a townhouse from Caesar's period, and at the very bottom water flows along the cloaca massima, by means of which the Etruscans dried out a swamp nearly 3,000 years ago – the prerequisite for building the Forum Romanum. *Mon–Sat 9am–12.30pm, 3–6pm, Sun 12.15–6pm | admission 10 euros | Via Labicana 95 | Metro B Colosseo | tram 3 | ꛵ H10*

🟦 SAN PIETRO IN VINCOLI

The church is attractive, but many visitors only come to see Michelangelo's powerful and magisterial figure of *Moses* (1516) on the tomb of Pope Julius II. The dynamic marble sculpture has enthralled psychologists like Sigmund Freud alongside generations of art lovers. It depicts Moses who, shaking with anger, has just caught his followers dancing around the Golden Calf. Moses is still seated, his hand fondling his long beard, yet he is about to stand with a display of his wrath. If he does the stone tablets bearing the Commandments seem likely to slip from his grasp and he appears to be trying to protect them … Michelangelo's genius has captured this gesture in marble.

The name of the church is derived from the chains *(vincoli)* with which St Peter is said to have been incarcerated in the Mamertine prison below the Capitol. They are kept as a precious relic below the high altar. *Daily 8am–12.30pm, 3–6pm | Piazza di San Pietro in Vincoli 4a | Metro B Cavour |* ⏱ *30 mins–1 hr | ⮞ G9*

🔟 SANTA MARIA MAGGIORE

Who says it never snows in Rome? Every year on the eve of 5 August in front of Santa Maria Maggiore flowers, scraps of paper or laser beams are used to create a spectacle in white to commemorate the founding of the church. On this evening in the year 352 the Virgin Mary is said to have instructed Pope Liberius to build a church on a spot on the Esquiline Hill where, the next morning, he would find snow. This is a genuinely impressive church and, incidentally, it was the first basilica that Pope Francis visited in 2013 after his election.

The patriarchal basilica is not only the largest *(maggiore)* of the 80 churches in Rome dedicated to the Virgin Mary, but its belltower is the city's tallest. Behind the lively Rococo façade are several treasures: the gleaming golden mosaics in the nave and on the chancel arch as well as the stone mosaic floors are among the finest in Rome. One thing emerges to spoil all this: the coffered ceiling from the time of the Borgia popes was covered in the first gold that the Spanish conquerors robbed from the inhabitants of the newly discovered American continents. *Daily 7am–7pm | Piazza Santa Maria Maggiore | bus 70, 71, 75 | ⮞ H8*

🔢 SAN GIOVANNI IN LATERANO

Quiz question: what is the most important church for Christianity? St Peter's? Wrong! It is the Lateran Basilica, which was consecrated in

San Giovanni in Laterano

Palazzo Montecitorio serves as the national parliament building

313 CE as a gift from Emperor Constantine to the then pope. It was anointed the "Mother of All Churches in the City and the World", as the inscription states on the outside. It was the seat of the pope for almost 1,000 years, until Pope Clement V went into exile in Avignon, Southern France in the 14th century.

The vast basilica, which always appears slightly sparse and empty, was modified during the baroque period. The cloister, a place of quiet retreat, and the baptistry are worth seeing. During the Holy Year 2016, many pilgrims came to the Lateran Basilica, and many were attracted to the *Scala Santa*, the Holy Steps, opposite. In memory of the suffering of Jesus, the pilgrims crawl (sounds painful) on their knees up the 28 steps

to the Sancta Sanctorum, the chapel for the popes. The steps were allegedly taken from the house of Pontius Pilate who had Jesus condemned to death on the cross. *Daily 7am–6.30pm, baptistery 7am–12.30pm | Piazza di San Giovanni in Laterano | Metro A S. Giovanni | bus 85, 87 | tram 3 | ⵌ J10–11*

🔟 PALAZZO MASSIMO ALLE TERME

Thousands of commuters and pedestrians, buses and taxis go past the Palazzo Massimo at Termini station every day without knowing what they are missing. The museum of antiquities shows the luxurious lifestyle of the rich and famous over the centuries, like a kind of historical *Hello* magazine. Rome's upper classes commissioned erotic frescoes to decorate the walls of their country villas, and erected majestic statues, such as the *Discus Thrower of Myron*, or art that still seems modern, like the *Sleeping Hermaphrodite*, in their villa gardens.

But the museum's highlight is the Painted Garden of the Villa of Livia, Rome's first Empress, displayed on the third floor. It's difficult to believe that the delicate frescoes are 2,000 years old; their original colours seem just as magically vibrant today. The wall frescoes depict a fantastical landscape in which everything is bursting into flower at once, with plants ignoring their usual seasonal cycles. Exotic birds flit about among slender cypresses, dark pine trees, bright red pomegranates and golden quinces. This is the hall where the imperial couple, Livia and Augustus, dined whenever they had had enough of Rome's exhausting political life. *Tue-Sun 9am-7.45pm | admission 7 euros (also for Palazzo Altemps, Terme di Diocleciano and Crypta Balbi, valid 3 days) | Largo di Villa Peretti 1 | Metro A, B Termini | □□ H8*

🔢 TERME DI DIOCLEZIANO

Opposite Stazione Termini lie the largest baths of Ancient Rome, which today belong to the *Museo Nazionale Romano*. Emperor Diocletian dedicated this temple to hygiene and relaxation in 306 CE, with huge water basins and baths for 2,400 visitors. In the baroque period a

Carthusian monastery designed by Michelangelo and the church of *Santa Maria degli Angeli* were constructed over the ruins of the baths. In the *Chiostro di Michelangelo* a large collection of sculpture and tablets harks back to the baths' ancient origins. *Daily 9am-7.45pm | admission 7 euros (also valid for Palazzo Altemps, Palazzo Massimo and Crypta Balbi) | entrance Via Enrico de Nicola 79 (near Stazione Termini) | Metro A, B Termini, Piazza dei Cinquecento| □□ H7*

SOUTHERN CENTRO STORICO

The heart of the historic city, the *Centro Storico* with its Renaissance and baroque palaces, theatrical squares, gushing fountains and wonky alleys, lies between Via del Corso, Piazza Venezia and the bend in the Tiber.

This is also the political epicentre of Italy. Piazza Colonna, where the Column of Marcus Aurelius tells of victories in battle against the Marcomanni, is the site of Palazzo Chigi, the Prime Minister's residence.

Behind it, on Piazza Montecitorio, is the national parliament, whose recent members have not always been known for their glorious deeds. Since 1946 the country has had 66 prime ministers. A walk through the narrow streets will almost automatically bring you to Piazza Navona, a baroque arena for people-watching, and to the Campo de' Fiori. In recent times not everything has been rosy in the heart of Rome. Exorbitant rents have driven out many of the old residents, and the ironsmiths and basket weavers can't keep their heads above water against the rising tide of fashion boutiques.

15 CAMPO DE' FIORI ⚑

A place to party! This is the piazza for meeting up in the evening and is especially popular with young people. In the middle of the square, surrounded by tall and restored palazzi, stands a memorial to the Dominican monk, Giordano Bruno, who was burned at the stake here during the Inquisition at the start of the Holy Year of 1600. From beneath his hood Bruno looks defiantly towards the Vatican, past the lively goings-on of the market in the morning and the party people and restaurant-goers in the evening.

The fruit and veg market has dwindled in recent years as the competition from supermarkets has taken its toll. However, many Romans still swear by the Campo, where they continue to buy their greens, root vegetables, spices and even clothes. Not many flowers are on sale, though, despite the name of the square, which in fact comes from the flower-filled meadow that was here in the Middle Ages. *Bus 40, 62, 63, 64 | ⧉ D9*

16 PALAZZO FARNESE

The elegant Palazzo Farnese near Campo de' Fiori is occupied by the French Embassy. Usually, for *"securité"* reasons, it is not even possible to sneak a glance inside the courtyard, which was designed by Michelangelo

Campo de' Fiori: marketplace by day, party place by night

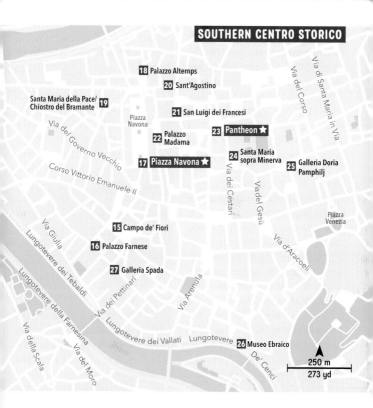

SOUTHERN CENTRO STORICO

18 Palazzo Altemps

20 Sant'Agostino

Santa Maria della Pace/
Chiostro del Bramante 19

Piazza
Navona

21 San Luigi dei Francesi

22 Palazzo
Madama

23 Pantheon ★

24 Santa Maria
sopra Minerva

25 Galleria Doria
Pamphilj

17 Piazza Navona ★

Via del Governo Vecchio

Corso Vittorio Emanuele II

Piazza
Venezia

15 Campo de' Fiori

16 Palazzo Farnese

27 Galleria Spada

26 Museo Ebraico

250 m
273 yd

in 1546. The gallery with famous frescoes by Annibale Carracci is being restored, but you can join one of the guided tours organised by the French agency *Inventer Rome* (tel. *34 93 68 30 13 | inventerrome. com)* to see other parts of the palace, including Michelangelo's divine staircase. *Piazza Farnese 67 | bus 40, 62, 64 | ▥ D9*

17 PIAZZA NAVONA ★

This beautiful, lively and colourful yet intimate arena is not to be missed. Like so many of Rome's attractive squares and streets, it owes its existence to a Renaissance Pope. In order to please his beloved sister-in-law Olimpia, Innocent X (1644–55) not only ordered the construction of Palazzo Pamphilj, today the Brazilian Embassy, but also laid out this wonderful square for her as a gift. It was built on the site of the *Circo Agonale*, a Roman stadium from whose name slang-loving Romans derived the word *Navona*.

Until the late 18th century princes of the Church and patrician families enjoyed contests and horse races from the windows of their palaces. And to cool Romans down in the summer, the piazza was flooded in August so that miniature naval battles could be staged. This baroque arena still functions as a stage for poor buskers and wealthy show-offs, mediocre artists and street hawkers, and well-known people about town with their mutts who trot past the busy tables of the cafés.

But the centre of attention on the piazza is Gianlorenzo Bernini's *Fontana dei Quattro Fiumi*. Four river gods are seated on a rocky grotto crowned by an obelisk. They represent the Danube, Nile, Ganges and Río de la Plata. The last of these has taken up such a defensive posture that he seems to be afraid that the church of Sant'Agnese opposite is about to collapse – and indeed, the church was designed by Bernini's rival Francesco Borromini. This is, however, a myth, as the baroque church was built two years after completion of the fountain. Bus 40, 64, 70, 81, 492

18 PALAZZO ALTEMPS

His Excellency had one simple rule when it came to taste: nothing but the best. In 1568 the Austrian Cardinal Hohenems, who became Cardinale Altemps, acquired a palazzo adjacent to Piazza Navona. He furnished the building with the very best that the art world had to offer: the frescoes and the wooden-panelled ceilings of the palazzo, and the loggia in the courtyard are impressive enough. But it's the marble statues of Aphrodite, Apollo, Hermes and Ares from the Ludovisi Collection which have cast a spell over generations of visitors.

Tue–Sun 9am–7.30pm | admission 7 euros (ticket includes Palazzo Massimo, Crypta Balbi and Terme di Diocleciano, valid for 3 days) | Piazza Sant' Appollinare 46 | bus 70, 81, 492 | ⏱ *1 hr |* ▥ *D8*

19 SANTA MARIA DELLA PACE/CHIOSTRO DEL BRAMANTE

Cloisters, Christian art and a café with great coffee makes for a pretty good mix. In the ★ *Caffetteria Chiostro del Bramante (see p. 82)* on the first floor, you sit directly above the Renaissance cloister created by Florentine star artist Donatello Bramante. Before or after you enjoy a cappuccino you can visit one of the temporary exhibitions in the *Chiostro del Bramante* cultural

The Neptune Fountain is a focal point in lively Piazza Navona

centre *(daily 10am–8pm | Arco della Pace 5)*. Santa Maria della Pace is next door. Although rarely open, it is worth visiting for Raphael's wonderful fresco depiction of the Sybils, Ancient Rome's fortune tellers *(in theory, but not confirmed, 9–11am and 3–5pm) Via della Pace 5 | bus 30, 40, 62, 64, 70, 492 | ▥ D8*

⑳ SANT'AGOSTINO

Sant'Agostino is a church for women. For centuries, expectant mothers have prayed for a smooth birth at the feet of the classically beautiful statue of *La Madonna del Parto* (*parto* means childbirth), created by the Florentine sculptor Jacopo Sansovino in 1541. In the days when it was common for young mothers (and their babies) to die during childbirth, this would have been a vital mission. Even today, many pregnant women drop in to say a quick prayer to the Madonna. Otherwise, they send their mothers or their grandmothers who, often dressed in black, linger in silent prayer to the Virgin Mary. Don't miss the painting *Madonna di Loreto* (Pilgrim's Madonna) in the first chapel to the left of the altar. This painting was created by the infamous Caravaggio in 1605 in his dramatic chiaroscuro style. Both his art and life frequently fluctuated between light and dark. *Daily 7.45am–12.30pm, 4–7.30pm | Piazza Sant'Agostino | bus 70, 81, 116, 492 | ▥ D8*

21 SAN LUIGI DEI FRANCESI

If you want to find out more about the "bad boy" of the baroque period, walk the 300m to the church of *San Luigi dei Francesi*. Often drunk, the ruffian Caravaggio was on the run from the Vatican police once again when the French granted him a safe hiding place here. He repaid the small French church's favour with the tremendous gift of three masterworks. However, the dramatic scenes from the life of Matthew caused a scandal because the disrespectful Caravaggio had created semi-naked portraits showing the saint as rather too human. *Daily 10am–12.30pm, Fri–Wed also 3–7pm | Piazza S. Luigi dei Francesi (behind Palazzo Madama) | bus 70, 81, 87, 492 | ⒨ D8*

22 PALAZZO MADAMA

Pope Clement VII (1523–34) de' Medici demonstrated his mastery of the art of diplomacy by marrying his illegitimate son Alessandro to the illegitimate daughter of Emperor Charles V. "Madama", as she was fondly called by the people of Rome, only lived in this Renaissance palace for a year before her husband was murdered. After that she had a career of her own. Her half-brother King Philip II made her governor of the Netherlands in recognition of her sharp mind. Incidentally, Pope Clement himself was also illegitimate. *Tutto in familia* – "it runs in the family" – as the Italians say. Since 1871 the palazzo has been home to the Italian senate. *Piazza Madama | bus 70, 81, 87, 492 | ⒨ D8*

23 PANTHEON ★

A cylinder with a dome on top: the Pantheon, built in 27 BCE at the behest of Marcus Agrippa, the son-in-law of Augustus, to honour all the gods, is a seemingly simple construction. The old Pantheon burned down twice before Emperor Hadrian rebuilt it in its current stunning form. From the outside, the 2,000-year-old temple looks slightly grey and pockmarked, but when you walk through the high, bronze doors your breath will be taken away as the ancient world's largest unsupported dome rises above you with its giant, open skylight. On sunny days, the effects of light are astonishing, and even more so **INSIDER TIP** *Ancient lightshow* if it rains, when water drains through a recess at the centre of the building. Why does this ancient temple – which was converted into a church in the Middle Ages and requisitioned as a memorial space for the Italian royal

Santa Maria sopra Minerva is the only Gothic church in Rome

family – lie conveniently for tourists at ground level, when in the age of Classical Rome, it was entered by ascending five steps? Over the centuries, the city accumulated 6m of rubble, and so its ancient buildings appear to have sunk. *Mon–Sat 8.30am–7.30pm, Sun 9am–6pm | free admission | Piazza della Rotonda | bus 40, 62, 64 | ▥ E8*

24 SANTA MARIA SOPRA MINERVA

Not all elephants are huge! In front of the church of *Santa Maria Sopra Minerva* stands a miniature elephant with an enormous saddle. The sculpture by the baroque artist Bernini is affectionately known as "Minerva's Chick". The little pachyderm also carries an ancient Egyptian obelisk, over 5m high, on its back. As though that were not enough of a burden, revellers have now also broken off one of his tusks – much to the horror of many Romans.

This, the only Gothic church in Rome, was built for the Dominican order in 1280 above the ruins of a temple dedicated to Minerva. To the left of the altar is Michelangelo's powerful figure of *Christ the Redeemer* (1521) holding the cross and the instruments of his martyrdom; the bronze loincloth was welded on later. The Cappella Caraffa in the south transept holds famous frescoes by Filippo Lippi that recount the life of St Thomas Aquinas (1492). *Daily 8am–7pm | Piazza della Minerva | bus 40, 62, 64*

25 GALLERIA DORIA PAMPHILJ

If you want to know how decadently Rome's aristocracy lived and how they splurged their wealth, make sure you visit the Palazzo Doria Pamphilj. The Rococo façade of the Palazzo on the Via del Corso has recently been renovated. Behind the façade are hundreds of rooms and a gallery decorated with gold and frescoes on walls of silk wallpaper, alongside artworks by Titian and Velázquez hung in rows, sometimes three paintings one above the other. Also on show is the famous portrait of the Pamphilj Pope Innocent X, who was anything but a devout and benign father of the church. He was famously led astray by his extravagant sister-in-law, Donna Olimpia (in fact his mistress). Plebs like us can get into the palace thanks to Jonathan Pamphilj, the heir to one of Italy's richest families, who has opened it to the public. *Daily 9am–7pm | admission 12 euros | Via del Corso 305 | doriapamphilj.it | bus 62, 63, 83, 85 | ○ 1–2 hrs | ▭ E8*

INSIDER TIP
Not a bad gaff

26 MUSEO EBRAICO

The Jewish quarter lies at the heart of Rome. It has seen boom times and tragedy. Today, it is a popular and lively quarter where Jewish tradition and kosher cuisine thrive once again.

The old synagogue is now open to all as the Museo Ebraico

The first Jews settled here as early as the second century BCE, which puts them among the true *romani romani*, the oldest citizens of Rome. Roman law granted them equality and religious freedom for centuries, until the missionary zeal of the Christians made them a persecuted minority. In the Middle Ages and baroque era they suffered under narrow-minded popes, who made them race against horses along Via del Corso as a popular amusement. In 1555 Pope Paul IV built a wall around the ghetto, and this confinement was not lifted until the unifying of the republic in 1870. However, the worst day in the ghetto was 16 October 1943, when the Gestapo herded 2,091 Jews onto trucks at the Portico d'Ottavia and deported them to death camps. Entire families were wiped out. Only 16 survivors, and only one woman, returned.

INSIDER TIP
Party with turtles

Around the popular *Fontana delle Tartarughe*, or Turtle Fountain, by Taddeo Landini, there is always a party atmosphere in the evenings. The fountain depicts four adolescents helping bronze turtles drink from the basin. The Roman *Teatro Marcello*, which was begun by Julius Caesar and completed by his successor Augustus, is now an archaeology park, and in summer classical concerts are held here. In the old synagogue the *Museo Ebraico (June–Sept 10am–5pm, Fri 9am–2pm; Oct–May Sun–Thu 9.30am–4.30pm | admission 11 euros | Lungotevere Cenci | museoebraico.roma.it)* displays precious silver items and robes, and organises guided tours through the ghetto. *Bus 23, 63, H, 280, Tram 8 | ⬚ E9*

27 GALLERIA SPADA

The 1540 palazzo is itself a masterpiece of playful Italian architecture. In the courtyard allow yourself to be baffled by the play on perspectives that Francesco Borromini designed for Cardinal Bernardino Spada. The statue of Mars appears to be large and some distance away from you, but the passageway is in reality only 9m long and the statue just 1m high. The optical illusion was achieved by decreasing the size of the columns behind it. The upper floor is home to an excellent collection of paintings by 17th- and 18th-centuries stars such as Annibale Carracci, Titian, Guido Reni, Domenichino and Caravaggio. *Wed–Mon 8.30am–7pm | admission 6 euros | Piazza Capo di Ferro 13 | galleria spada.beniculturali.it | bus 62, 64 | ⏱ 1 hr | ⬚ D9*

NORTHERN CENTRO STORICO

The fashion quarter between the Spanish Steps and Via del Corso offers plenty of haute couture shopping with lots of *alta moda* boutiques housed in old palazzi – making them seem even more glamorous!

Via del Corso, once home to the English Romantic poet Percy Bysshe Shelley , used to be a shopping strip popular with young people for its cheap clothing. Now, new luxury boutiques, like that of the five Fendi sisters, invite you to splurge on some high-class shopping. The most exclusive streets are Via Condotti and Via del Babuino, and the cheapest is Via del Tritone. If you've had enough retail therapy, stop by the Trevi Fountain or pay a visit to the president in the Quirinal Palace. If he is not there to receive you, you can get over the snub thanks to view from the piazza with the Dioscuri.

28 FONTANA DI TREVI (TREVI FOUNTAIN) ★

The scene from the film *La Dolce Vita* is legendary and is one reason why the Trevi Fountain has become globally famous. However, on that ice-cold February evening in 1960 when Marcello Mastroianni, who was then Italy's top film star, was supposed to climb into the fountain with Anita Ekberg, life was anything but sweet. The film was almost a flop. The Swedish actress was used to the chilly waters of the Baltic Sea, but her partner Mastroianni, often typecast as a Latin lover, emerged as an Italian wimp and refused to get into the fountain. Only when star director, Federico Fellini, agreed to let him wear hip-high angler's waders beneath his black trousers and dinner jacket were they able to shoot the scene – and the myth

INSIDER TIP
Cinematic ice bath

was born of the everlasting *dolce vita* in Rome. In 2016, none of the models got cold feet during Karl Lagerfeld's fashion show, thanks to an almost invisible glass platform he had had constructed in the fountain.

Built in 1750, the Fontana di Trevi depicts the god of sea, Oceanus, ruling over the waves while Tritons tame his horses. It is not only thanks to the fountain's illustrious past or its baroque grandeur that tourists from all over the world swarm around it 24 hours a day. Most people just lob a coin into the water, thinking it will bring them back to Rome some time. Who knows? Maybe it will. *Piazza di Trevi | bus 62, 63, 81, 85, 95, 492 | F8*

29 SCALINATA DI TRINITÀ DEI MONTI (SPANISH STEPS) ★ ⚑

The Spanish Steps always have always been a favourite place for visitors to Rome. Unfortunately, this has its disadvantages. In the late 18th century, English poets like John Keats and Shelley could sit quietly writing their poetry on the curved balustrades that were designed by Alessandro Specchi and Francesco di Sanctis in 1723. Today, the wide steps are filled with young Romans and tourists, even though drinking, picnicking, smoking weed and playing guitar are officially banned. However, flirting is allowed.

The popularity of the steps led to a huge increase in rubbish, largely from fast-food restaurants. The jeweller Bulgari, whose luxury store is just next door and looks on to them, recently paid 1.5 million euros for the restoration of the elegant *scalinata*. A sticky mass of burger, pizza and chewing gum was removed, along with red wine and ketchup stains. Bulgari also restored the tinkling *Fontana della Barcaccia*, the boat-shaped fountain, designed in 1629 by Pietro Bernini, the father of the even more famous sculptor Gianlorenzo Bernini. It now flows crystal clear at the foot of the Spanish Steps. Nevertheless, on Rome's favourite square litter continues to build up. *Metro A Spagna* | ⛁ *E-F7*

The best known staircase in Rome is the Scalinata di Trinità dei Monti, or the Spanish Steps

30 ARA PACIS AUGUSTAE

An ultra-modern construction of steel and glass surrounds Emperor Augustus's 2,000-year-old Altar of Peace. This project by the American architect Richard Meier drew a barrage of criticism reminiscent of the reaction to the glass pyramid at the Louvre in Paris. But after ten years of complaints and protests, the people of Rome have come to accept it. Directly opposite lies the *Mausoleo di Augusto*, commissioned by the emperor himself and built in 27 BCE, even though Augustus went on to rule for a further 41 years. *Tue–Sun 9am–7pm | admission 10.50 euros | Lungotevere in Augusta | bus 70, 81 |* ⏱ *½-1 hr |* 🕮 *E7*

31 CASA DI GOETHE

What does Andy Warhol have to do with Goethe? Goethe's famous portrait in the Roman Campagna and its colourful Pop Art version by Warhol are both displayed in the cultural forum at the Casa di Goethe in Rome. An Italophile who spent 15 months in Rome between 1786 and 1787, Goethe once said "O, how happy I feel in Rome when I think of the times when a grey day back in the north would wrap around me". Indeed, during his time here, he adopted an Italian alias, Filippo Möller. The apartment that he shared with his painter friend Heinrich W Tischbein has been a museum and cultural

INSIDER TIP
Goethe: the very first influencer?

The ancient Ara Pacis is topped by Richard Meier's modern museum building

NORTHERN CENTRO STORICO

37 Museo Nazionale Etrusco di Villa Giulia

Bioparco

36 Galleria Nazionale d'Arte Moderna

Giardino d. Lago

Galleria Borghese ★ **35**

Piazza di Siena

34 Villa Borghese

32 Santa Maria del Popolo
33 Pincio/Piazza del Popolo

Galoppatoio

Corso d'Italia

31 Casa di Goethe

30 Ara Pacis Augustae

Piazza di Spagna

29 **Scalinata di Trinità dei Monti (Spanish Steps)** ★

38 Capuchin Crypt (Museo dei Padri Cappuccini)

Piazza Parlamento

Fontana di Trevi (Trevi Fountain) ★ **28**

Giardino del Quirinale

39 San Carlo
40 Sant'Andrea al Quirinale

500 m
547 yd

Piazza Navona

Scuderie del Quirinale **41**

venue for 20 years now. *Tue-Sun 10am-6pm | admission 5 euros | Via del Corso 18 | casadigoethe.it | bus 117, 119 | ▢ E6*

32 SANTA MARIA DEL POPOLO

The pilgrim to Rome and later proclaimer of the Reformation Martin Luther celebrated mass here with his fellow Augustinian monks in 1510 before he rejected papacy and the Catholic confession. The beautiful church, which is just behind the Porta del Popolo, was constructed in the 11th century to exorcize Nero's evil spirit that supposedly haunted the place. Inside, visitors are treated to an artistic feast: the frescoes in the choir and Cappella Rovere are by Pinturicchio; in the Cappella Cerasi, to the left of the altar, are the *Conversion of St Paul* and *Crucifixion of St Peter* by Caravaggio, the genius and bad boy of the baroque period. The Cappella

Chigi, the second from the right, was decorated by Raphael for a family of bankers; in the choir are two tombs by Andrea Sansovino; the marble figures of the high altar depicting the *Madonna del Popolo* are the work of Bernini and Lorenzetto. That's quite a list of famous artists. *Mon–Fri 7.30am–12pm, 4–7pm, Sat 7am–7pm Sun 8am–1.30pm, 4.30–7pm | Piazza del Popolo 12 | Metro A Flaminio | Ⅲ E6*

🔢 PINCIO/PIAZZA DEL POPOLO

It's hard to think of anything more romantic than watching the sun go down over the roofs of Rome from the Pincio. On the piazza below are the twin churches of *Santa Maria dei Miracoli* and *Santa Maria in Montesanto*, which look more interesting from the hilltop than they do from inside. *The Piazza del Popolo* was once a kind of Roman reception area for all the pilgrims and travellers entering the Eternal City from the Via Cassia or Via Flaminia. When Queen Christina of Sweden appeared at the gates in 1655, Bernini had just finished altering Michelangelo's gateway into the elegant form it has today. The Piazza of the People (*popolo* means people) is now a meeting point for demonstrations and protest marches, as the buses filled with demonstrators can easily park outside the Porta del Popolo. In the distance, you can see the green shores of the River Tiber and Michelangelo's dome of San Pietro. *Metro A Spagna, Flaminio | Ⅲ E6*

Park Villa Borghese: Rome's green lungs, complete with temple, stream and nature park

34 VILLA BORGHESE 👥

This majestic park plays a vital role in many Romans' happy childhood memories. It is where they played football with their fathers, learned to ride ponies, or glid across the *laghetto*, the small lake, in a rowing boat. Today, the park is popular with joggers, cyclists and rickshaw riders; Segways also glide almost silently through the avenues of cypress trees. You can simply relax on a bench in the sunshine and listen to the small fountain or the ringtones of your neighbours on the bench. You can even go online, as the Villa Borghese has free Wi-Fi zones. In May, an equestrian tournament is held at the *Piazza di Siena*. At the northern end of the park the former zoo is now an ecological park *(April-Oct daily 9.30am-7pm; otherwise 9.30am-5pm | admission 15 euros)* with many native animals, from frogs to a Capitoline Wolf. *Via Pinciana | bus 52, 53, 490, 495 | tram 3, 19 | 🗺 F5*

35 GALLERIA BORGHESE ★

Miracles happen, but in the Eternal City it can take a while. After a 17-year restoration, Cardinal Scipione Borghese's baroque pleasure palace has finally reopened. The prelate was one of the world's greatest art patrons. Ever since it reopened there has been a rush for tickets (only available online). On the ground floor you will see Bernini's sculptures *Daphne and Apollo*, *David*, *The Rape of Proserpina* and Antonio Canova's semi-nude statue of *Paolina Borghese*, Napoleon's sister.

On the first floor, you'll find works by the artists Lucas Cranach, Titian, Paul Veronese, Raphael, Peter Paul Rubens and Caravaggio. *Tue–Sun 8.30am-7.30pm | admission 15 euros| registration only galleria borgheseticket.it | Piazza Scipione Borghese 5 | bus 52, 53, 490 | ⏱ 2 hrs | 🗺 G5*

36 GALLERIA NAZIONALE D'ARTE MODERNA

Modern art has a tough time in a city that is so saturated with historic attractions. Nevertheless, the curators here have put together an amazing collection of 19th- and 20th-century paintings and sculptures, including works by Giorgio de Chirico, Gustav Klimt, Vincent van Gogh, Henry Moore, Picasso, Mondrian and Jackson Pollock. The white palazzo was built in 1911 for the International Exhibition of Art in Rome. The rooms are light and the Villa Borghese Park is next door. The well-stocked museum shop has an entertaining selection: *Libreria Gnam. Tue–Sun 8.30am-7.30pm | admission 13 euros | Viale delle Belle Arti 131 | gnam.beniculturali.it | tram/ bus 3, 19 | 🗺 E-F4*

37 MUSEO NAZIONALE ETRUSCO DI VILLA GIULIA

Why the cool smile? *Apollo di Veio*, the 2,500-year-old highlight of the Etruscan museum, looks even more attractive than before his rejuvenation. His most recent facelift hit the headlines as the restoration was paid for by a tobacco company that wanted to enhance its less-than-glamorous image by sponsoring culture. However, the deal has succeeded in sending visitor numbers to the previously sleepy museum through the roof.

The elegant Villa Giulia, like many other Roman villas, was a summer residence the 16th-century Pope Julius III. For more than a hundred years the villa has housed finds from necropolises, the Etruscan grave sites in Latium, Umbria and Tuscany. The most moving exhibit is the *Sarcofago degli Sposi*, the tomb of a married couple from the sixth century BCE. The ancient couple look stress-free and radiate more harmony and devotion than many contemporary couples. What would they think if they knew that many of their lavish grave goods, golden necklaces and rings would be copied and sold today as modern jewellery? *Tue–Sun 8.30am–7.30pm | admission 8 euros | Piazzale di Villa Giulia 9 | villagiulia. beniculturali.it | tram/bus 3, 19 |* ⏱ *1–2 hrs |* ▥ *E4*

> **INSIDER TIP**
> **The happiest couple in the Ancient World**

❸ CAPUCHIN CRYPT (MUSEO DEI PADRI CAPPUCCINI)

On Via Veneto you can visit a macabre but space-saving deathly vault: skull piled on skull, bone on bone. Capuchin monks buried some 4,000 of their brothers in this crypt beneath *Santa Maria della Concezione. Daily 9am–7pm | admission 8.50 euros | Via Veneto 27 | bus 52, 63, 83 |* ▥ *F7*

❸ SAN CARLO

Borromini began this baroque jewel with its oval dome in 1638. It was still not finished when he died in 1667. The concave and convex curves of its façade and the eagle sculpture are some of the great architect's masterpieces. *Mon–Fri 10am–6pm, Sat 10am–1pm, Sun 12–1pm | Via del Quirinale 23/Via delle Quattro Fontane | bus 40, 64, 70 |* ▥ *X0*

❹ SANT'ANDREA AL QUIRINALE

A beauty contest for churches! Only a few steps away from San Carlo you can visit this church built by Borromini's great rival, Bernini. This is a popular church for weddings with its unusual layout (like a posh living room in old rose, gold and white). *Tue–Sun 8.30am–12pm, 2.30–6pm | Via del Quirinale 29 | f G8*

❹ SCUDERIE DEL QUIRINALE

Where once horses whinnied in the papal stables, there is now a gallery with great temporary exhibitions. After visiting an exhibition, make sure you stop and admire the superb view from the staircase that looks out over domes, churches and roof gardens. *Opening times vary by exhibition | Via XXIV Maggio 16 | scuderiequirinale.it | bus 60, 64, 70, 71, 170 |* ▥ *F8*

> **INSIDER TIP**
> **Staircase with a view**

Priestly ordination in San Pietro, the centre of the Catholic world

PAPAL ROME

At 44 hectares, the Vatican may be little bigger than an average-sized farm but the smallest country in the world is the centre of a religion with more than a billion followers.

Once this state spread out across much of central Italy. Today's 572 inhabitants don't want for anything – they don't even have to pay tax and literacy is 100% (even if population growth is 0%). The Swiss Guard is the oldest and smallest army in the world. There are 110 soldiers, of whom 78 are on limited contracts. They must be young, single, Catholic and Swiss . And it is rumoured that well-defined calves boost your chances.

The Vatican also has its own railway – the world's smallest, with 400m of track, one platform, one set of points but no trains. Should it need to run, Italy's state railway will provide the necessaries. But in the last 88 years, only four popes have set off from the grand Vatican station. If you would like to get more than a fleeting impression of the Vatican with St Peter's Basilica, St Peter's Square and the Castel Sant'Angelo, allow plenty of time. The Vatican Museums, including the Sistine Chapel, are not only home to the world's greatest collection of art treasures: in the tourist season they also have the longest queues. Patience, as they say, is a virtue!

42 SAN PIETRO (ST PETER'S) ★

St Peter's Basilica can only be described with superlatives. It is Europe's biggest church, measuring 211m in length, 186m at its widest point and 132m at its highest. It can hold 60,000 worshippers. In 1506 Pope Julius II gave Donato Bramante the task of building a new church to replace the ancient basilica that Emperor Constantine had erected over the tomb of St Peter. In the 120-year period of construction, the best architects in Italy came up with many mutually contradictory models: Bramante wanted the floorplan of a Greek cross with a massive dome but, to meet the wishes of later popes, this was changed to a cross with one longer arm. The nave had not been completed when Michelangelo took up Bramante's ideas again in 1546 and started the construction of a large dome on the model of the cathedral in Florence. Pope Paul V in turn wanted St Peter's to have the longest nave of any Christian church and awarded Carlo Maderno the commission to extend it and design the façade, which, however, restricted the view of the dome.

The Porta Santa, or Holy Door, is on the right when you enter the church

VATICAN CURIOSITIES

What is an *ipsophonum*?

Catholics come to Rome from all over the world – how on earth do they communicate with each other in their holiest place? It's easy: they speak Latin, the official Vatican language. The problem is that classical Latin lacks words for many contemporary things. Since 1976 there has been a New Latin dictionary in which an answering machine is called an *ipsophonum*, a mobile phone is a *telephonum manuale* and a cash machine is an *automata monetalia*. However, as so few people really speak fluent Latin, Italian, the second official language, is often preferred.

Popemobile

Pope John Paul II was the first Pope to use the popemobile on his official visits. One accompanied him on all his 104 trips so he could be as close as possible to the faithful. Most of the 60 papal vehicles remained in the host countries and have been re-used in subsequent visits. The current popemobile is a converted Mercedes M-Class with a top speed of just 80 mh. The number plate "SCV" of all Vatican official vehicles stands for **S**tato della **C**ittà del **V**aticano – Vatican City State – although many Italians prefer to interpret it as **S**e **C**risto lo **V**edesse – if Christ were to see that …

PAPAL ROME

44 Vatican Museums (Musei Vaticani)

Via Crescenzio

45 Vatican Gardens (Giardini Vaticani)

Borgo Vittorio

📍 Cappella Sistina ★

Castel Sant'Angelo 46
(Castle of the Holy Angel)

San Pietro (St Peter's) ★ 42

*Piazza
San Pietro*

43 Campo Santo Teutonico

Galleria Nazionale 48
Villa Farnesina

47 Gianicolo

500 m
547 yd

and is only opened in special years – the last time was when Pope Francis declared a Holy Year in 2016. Michelangelo's *Pietà* is protected by bullet-proof glass in the first chapel on the right, as in 1972 someone smashed its nose. On the pillar dedicated to St Longinius, the foot of a bronze statue of St Peter has been polished to a shine by the kisses of pilgrims. Marble steps in front of the papal altar lead down to the tomb of St Peter and the last resting place of Pope John Paul II. Above them stands the bronze baldachin designed by Bernini. The visitor entrance to the papal tombs and the Vatican catacombs is on the right-hand side of the church.

> **INSIDER TIP**
> **Mary behind reinforced glass**

Two further works by Bernini are in the apse: the cathedral altar with the papal throne and the tomb of Urban VIII, a pope from the Barberini family. On the left in the nave is the entrance to the sacristy and the Vatican treasury.

The lift to the roof is on the right of the church (turn right at the bronze door) where you'll find a nice café and souvenir shop. After that 320 steep steps lead up to the dome, from where the view of Rome is superb (if you don't suffer from vertigo). Be sure to wear decent clothing, i.e. long trousers and no uncovered shoulders! *Church daily 7am–7pm; winter 7am–6.30pm, sacristy 9am–6pm; winter 9am–5pm |*

> **INSIDER TIP**
> **Cappuccino on Cathlicism's roof**

admission 5 euros; roof and dome 8am–6pm; winter 9am–5pm | admission 5 euros, with lift 7 euros | security checks beneath the right-hand colonnade | Metro A Ottaviano | bus 40, 62, 64 | ⏱ 2-3 hrs | ⍟ A–B7

🟥 CAMPO SANTO TEUTONICO

This small oasis is a space of commemoration for the Germans in Rome. The entrance is behind the left-hand colonnade of St Peter's, and if you say the magic words "Campo Santo Teutonico", the Swiss Guard will let you through. The little cemetery in front of the Collegio Teutonico is the last resting place of writers like Stefan Andres, the archaeologist Ludwig Curtius and many German pilgrims who reached Rome and never returned home. *Daily 7am–noon | Via della Sagrestia 17 | bus 40, 64 | ⍟ A8*

🟥 VATICAN MUSEUMS (MUSEI VATICANI)

What are all these people doing here? Unfortunately, you are not the only visitor to the largest and finest museum complex in the world! Almost 5 million people make the pilgrimage every year through the 13 museums to see the ultimate highlight and reward for the crowds: the famous Sistine Chapel.

Here are four tips on how to view the Vatican Museums: 1) Book online. With queues stretching for miles along the walls, you'd be silly not to. 2) Be careful of touts. There are some people who spend a small fortune, about 2,220 euros, to see Michelangelo's frescoes without the crowds. There are also exclusive group tours and official fast-track tickets are available at 7.30am from 56 euros. However, polyglot touts may approach you in the queue to rip you off with offers such as "Sixtine Chapel fast track"… Keep well clear! 3) The best time to visit? Tuesday and Thursday are generally the quietest days, and Wednesday morning, when the Pope holds a general audience on St Peter's Square, is also good. Avoid Monday when the Vatican is twice as full because Rome's national museums are closed. 🐦 If you don't mind crowds and have plenty of patience you should come on the last Sunday of the month when admission is free. 4) The (only) entrance to the museums is not inside St Peter's, as many tourists wrongly believe, but at Viale del Vaticano on the north side of the Vatican complex, about ten minutes on foot from St Peter's Square.

At last it's time to get stuck in! The unique art obstacle course, which includes 13 museums with about 50,000 objects, is 7km! There are several highlights you shouldn't miss even if you are keen to make headway to the Sistine Chapel. The *Museo Pio Clementino* displays are the most beautiful and thrilling classical statues in the world (according to both archaeologists and art historians). For example, the Laocoön Group in the Cortile del Belvedere. This marble ensemble (second century BCE) shows the Priest Laocoön with his two sons in a dramatic battle with a giant serpent that the Greek Goddess Athena has sent them as a punishment

The Vatican Museums hold around 50,000 works of art

because the priest wanted to warn the Trojans about the Greeks and their wooden horse.

Next, you will see probably the most handsome man in the Vatican, the *Apollo of Belvedere* (a Roman copy, second century, of the Greek original, fourth century BCE). The antique *Torso of Belvedere* is a little oblong figure of muscles without head, arms or legs, yet the majestic and dynamic rotation of the body is astonishing, and the torso became a model for many Renaissance artists, including Michelangelo. Another beauty is the

INSIDER TIP
Ancient amazing abs

Roman copy of the Venus of Knidos originally sculpted by the renowned Greek artist Praxiteles in the fourth century BCE.

If you follow the route through the *Pinacoteca Vaticana* you will find first-class paintings and sculptures from the Middle Ages to the 19th century. This is a VIP show of great artists like Giotto, Fra Angelico, Filippo Lippi, Lucas Cranach, Perugino, Leonardo da Vinci, Titian, Veronese, Caravaggio, van Dyck and Bernini. Have we forgotten anyone? You will be able to add the talented painter Pinturicchio after visiting the *Appartamento Borgia* where he decorated the rooms of the Borgia Pope Alexander VI with 86 murals from 1492–95. This was a dark period: here in 1500, the pope's son Cesare Borgia is said to have murdered his brother-in-law, Alfonso de Aragón, the husband of his sister Lucrezia.

You will find the grand master Raphael displayed in the *Stanze e Logge di Raffaello*. The four halls that Pope Julius II had decorated by him from 1508 are a highlight of Renaissance art. However, the glory of the beautiful frescoes didn't last for long. In 1527, during the *Sacco di Roma*, the sack of Rome, the papal apartments were heavily damaged by brutal Protestant rebels: faces were scratched away and graffiti promoting the Reformation were added. The damage is gradually being repaired.

INSIDER TIP
Raphael's selfie

The School of Athens fresco depicts philosophers Plato, Aristotle, Pythagoras and Diogenes in discussion. But Raphael couldn't resist including a self-portrait along with Michelangelo. This and the dramatic Fire in the Borgo gleam in their freshly restored state. The 12 arcades of the loggia are up next.

Finally you arrive where everyone wants to go: the ★ *Cappella Sistina (Sistine Chapel)*. Michelangelo's story of the creation in the papal chapel is resplendent in the almost Pop Art colours of lime green, pale purple and orange. The Renaissance genius – also known as *Il Divino*, "the divine one" – took four years (1508–12) to paint the ceiling frescoes alone whose total length is 41m. He worked with his head tilted backwards the whole time

(he must have had quite a stiff neck by the end!) and with a lighted candle on his hat. "My eye is bad, I am not fit to paint", Michelangelo had written to a friend. He would have preferred to create marble sculptures. What a bizarre thing to say. His story of the creation has incredible plasticity. The frescoes are unique artworks and relate the creation of light to the story of Adam and Eve and the fall of mankind, the flood and Noah, all framed by powerful sibyls and gloomy-looking prophets. Of the 340 biblical scenes, the *Creation of Adam*, on which the divine spark passes from hand to hand, is the most impressive and certainly the most often reproduced.

More than 20 years later, when Michelangelo was 60 years old, Pope Paul III commissioned him to paint *The Last Judgement* on the end wall of the chapel. When the finished work was unveiled at Christmas 1541, it caused a scandal: a naked Christ was revealed, gathering a whirl of equally naked saints around him with a regal gesture – the chosen, the resurrected and the damned. It was Michelangelo's superb final flourish. Rome was on the threshold of the Counter-Reformation and modern art lovers can count themselves lucky that the pious counter-reformers did not destroy the work immediately.

However, Michelangelo's pupil Daniele de Volterra was later

INSIDER TIP
Sinful Saints

obliged to paint some drapery around the saints' most saintly regions. But honour was eventually restored for

Michelangelo's masterpiece: the ceiling fresco in the Sistine Chapel

Il Divino; when *The Last Judgement* was restored in the 1990s and the restorers washed off 17 of the 40 loincloths. Incidentally, it is widely believed that the face painted on the flayed skin of St Bartholomew is actually a self-portrait of Michelangelo. *Mon–Sat 9am–6pm (last admission 4pm), last Sun in month 9am–2pm (last admission 12.30pm)* | *admission 16 euros, l last Sun in month free of charge* | *Evening opening (usually with small concerts performed by young prodigies) May–Oct Fri 7–9pm* | *17 euros plus 4 euros online charge (book well in advance)* | *museivaticani. va* | *guided tours (rome-museum.com, througheternity.com) available in English* | *Metro A Cipro–Musei Vaticani* | *bus 23, 32, 81* | 🚇 *A–B 6–7*

45 GIARDINI VATICANI (VATICAN GARDENS)

The green space of the Vatican: more than half the city-state's area consists of spacious gardens with manicured flower beds, cedars, palms and pine trees. Since the Argentinian Jorge Bergoglio (Pope Francis) has resided here, a colony of green monk parakeets also happens to have moved in. The South American parrots, which have probably escaped from a zoo, chatter and screech loudly, even when their countryman, the Holy Father, takes his daily walk. Incidentally, Pope Francis doesn't live in the majestic Vatican like his predecessors did. After the conclave he remained in the simple guesthouse at the centre of the garden.

The *Necropoli di Santa Rosa*, an ancient Roman burial ground, which was recently discovered beneath the Vatican car park, is only open to tour groups who apply in writing to the *Ufficio Visite Speciali Giardini Vaticani*

(visiteguidatesingoli.musei@scv.va). Gardens: two-hour guided tours only by prior registration at museivaticani. va | admission 32 euros, also valid for the Musei Vaticani | tel. 06 69 88 46 76 | ▥ A7

46 CASTEL SANT'ANGELO (CASTLE OF THE HOLY ANGEL)

This angelic fortification, a place of refuge for the popes, was built above the cylindrical mausoleum of Emperor Hadrian (117–138 CE). It owes its name to a legend dating from Christmas in the year 590, when, at the peak of a plague epidemic, the Archangel Michael appeared to Pope Gregory I and sheathed his sword. With this gesture the plague ended.

Since 1281 the castle has been connected to the Vatican Palace by a

La Chiocciola, or "the snail" is the name given to this staircase in the Vatican Museums

covered passage, the *Passetto*. Behind its strong walls are located magnificent apartments for the popes, storerooms and some less-than-angelic torture chambers for heretics too. In July and August, concerts take place on the roof terrace.

From the battlements you get a fantastic view of Rome's most beautiful bridge, the *Ponte Sant'Angelo*. Fortunately, it is only open to pedestrians, so you can admire Bernini's ten baroque angels in peace. *Tue–Sun 9am–7pm, Fri 9am–10pm | admission 10 euros | castelsantangelo.beniculturali.com | bus 23, 40, 62 | C7*

47 GIANICOLO

No high-rises spoil the view from the Gianicolo hill – dedicated to the two-faced god Janus – over the domes, churches and palaces of Rome. The hill is also home to the equestrian statue of Italian freedom fighter Giuseppe Garibaldi, the hero of the unification of Italy. In 1849 he fought against French troops on this hill. Alongside him is Anita Garibaldi, probably the only female rider statue in the world. *Discovery Tour "Green Rome: Trastevere, Gianicolo and the Tiber" (see p. 138) | Bus 75, 115, 870 | B–C 9–10*

48 GALLERIA NAZIONALE VILLA FARNESINA

The parties held in the small palazzo on the River Tiber were famous throughout the city, especially the very last one. After the banquet, the rich banker Agostini Chigi had the dirty silver cutlery thrown into the Tiber in front of his horrified guests. However, shrewd banker that he was, Chigi had arranged for the waiters to spread invisible underwater nets beforehand. As soon as the last guest had left, the expensive silver cutlery was fished out of the Tiber again.

The small Renaissance building dates from 1508 and was designed by the artist Baldassare Peruzzi who also painted the playful frescoes. But the fresco *Amor and Psyche* by the great master Raphael is in another league. The owner of the palazzo is said to have been his model until Chigi got a bit worried about the intimacy and expelled the genius. *Mon–Sat 9am–2pm | admission 6 euros | Via della Lungara 230 | villafarnesina.it | bus 23, 280 | C9*

TRASTEVERE & TESTACCIO

Trastevere, Rome's largest village *trans tiberim* ("across the Tiber"), as it was called in Augustus's day still has charm, even though it has perhaps been over-gentrified in recent years.

Houses here were built for artisans and are smaller and more modest than the grand palaces in the city centre. They are painted in traditional colours which light up at sunset to become bold reds, purples and yellows. Where once everyone knew everyone and old folk put their chairs on the pavement in the evening for a chat, an upmarket quarter with a big clubbing scene has emerged.

Neighbouring *Testaccio* – known by locals as the belly of Rome – once extremely quiet, also has a lively nightlife now that bars and clubs have opened in the former slaughterhouse. However, in these districts there are still many residents who would not sell their eccentric little apartments at any price. And many of those who have moved out come back each July for the *Festa de Noiantri* to party with old neighbours and friends.

49 MONTE TESTACCIO

The 39m Testaccio hill is made out of ceramic shards that are thousands of years old – around 53 million of them in total. This was the site of the wholesale market halls of Ancient Rome. As the traders packed their wares in

Despite gentrification and tourism, laundry still billows over the streets

TRASTEVERE & TESTACCIO

54 Street art on the Tiber

53 Tevere & Isola Tiberina

52 Santa Maria in Trastevere

51 Piazza dei Cavalieri di Malta

49 Monte Testaccio

Piramide di Cestio 50

500 m
547 yd

ceramic amphorae instead of bags, this historic tip grew up. The old slaughterhouse is now a cultural centre where the contemporary art gallery *MACRO Future (Piazza Orazio Giustinaini 4)* presents special exhibitions. Only guided tour groups can access Monte Testaccio *(to register, tel. 06 06 08)*. *Via Galvani/Via Zabaglia | Metro B Piramide | bus 170, 719, 781 | ⊞ D–E 12–13*

50 PIRAMIDE DI CESTIO

In ancient times Egypt with its pyramids and obelisks was highly fashionable. That is why the praetor and tribune Caius Cestius had himself buried like a little pharaoh in a luxury pyramid tomb in 11 BCE. The restoration of the ancient obelisk cost two million euros and was paid for by the Japanese fashion designer and patron Yuzo Yagi. Incidentally this was one of the few occasions that something happened ahead of schedule in the Eternal City: the renovation only took 322 days, 75 fewer than planned. *Piazza Ostiense | Metro B Piramide | tram 3 | bus 23, 60, 83 | ⊞ E12*

51 PIAZZA DEI CAVALIERI DI MALTA

A spot for romantics and key-hole peepers on the Aventine hill. In 1766 the architect and engraver Giovanni B Piranesi built the seat of the Order of

Centrale Montemartini

Knights of St John, which describes itself as a sovereign state and has its own car number plates, though it lacks its own territory. Peep through the iron-clad keyhole of the green wooden gate of no. 4, the ☞ *Buco di*

Roma – and you will get a perfectly framed view of St Peter's Basilica in the distance. *Metro B Circo Massimo | bus 30, 60, 75, 118, 175 | tram 3 | ⏎ E11*

52 SANTA MARIA IN TRASTEVERE

At night-time it is magically illuminated, but in daylight Rome's oldest Church of Our Lady glistens with the third-century gold mosaic *Mary and the Ten Holy Women* (12th century). The most beautiful mosaics are in the apse: an oversized Jesus with the Virgin and saints. *Daily 7.30am–8pm | Piazza S. Maria in Trastevere | bus H | tram 8 | ⏎ D10*

53 TEVERE & ISOLA TIBERINA

The Tevere, or Tiber, flows into Mediterranean 20km outside Rome near Ostia. It plays a big part in the myth about the founding of Rome as it is believed to be the river into which Romulus and Remus were thrown in a basket as infants. In antiquity the island in the River Tiber was dedicated to Aesculapius, the god of healing. Around the year 1000 the church of San Bartolomeo was built on the remains of a temple. The *Ospedale Fatebenefratelli* (in English "do good deeds, brothers") keeps up the medical tradition to this day. To reach the island, cross the *Ponte Fabrizio* and *Ponte Cestio*, the oldest and most beautiful of the 21 bridges across the Tiber. Today you can bask in the sun on a man-made beach or enjoy the walking and cycling lanes *(piste ciclabili, piste-cicla bili.com)* along the promenade. The most attractive section is from Ponte Sublicio to Ponte Milvio (10km). *E10*

54 STREET ART ON THE TIBER

The 550-m frieze, *Triumphs and Laments*, was etched into the washed walls along the Tiber by William Kentridge, a South African street artist, in 2016. The 80 grey and white images depict scenes from Roman history – from the Romulus to Caesar Augustus, and from Michelangelo and Mussolini to the 1975 murder of film director and poet Pier Paolo Pasolini. Unfortunately, less skilled graffiti has repeatedly vandalised the ensemble. "Every victory has a defeat", the artist said, and much the same can be said for street art. *Lungotevere della Farnesina zwischen Ponte Sisto und Ponte Mazzini | bus 30, 63, 280 | C–D9*

OUTSIDE THE CENTRE

55 CENTRALE MONTEMARTINI ★

A radiant white Venus, the Aphrodite of Knidos, Roman emperors, generals and philosophers in a former power station? Don't miss this unusual place to see heroes and gods. *Tue–Sun 9am–7pm | admission 7.50 euros, combined ticket with Musei Capitolini 16 euros | Via Ostiense 106 | Metro B Piramide or Garbatella | bus 716, tram/bus 3, bus 23 | E14*

56 CINECITTÀ

Do you remember the wild chariot race in the film *Ben-Hur* with knife blades on the spokes of the chariots

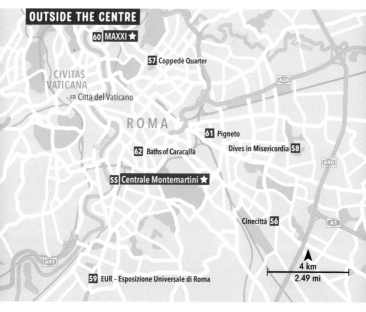

OUTSIDE THE CENTRE

60 MAXXI ★

57 Coppedè Quarter

CIVITAS VATICANA
⊞ Città del Vaticano

A24

ROMA

61 Pigneto

62 Baths of Caracalla

Dives in Misericordia 58

A90

55 Centrale Montemartini ★

Cinecittà 56

A1

A91

59 EUR - Esposizione Universale di Roma

4 km
2.49 mi

Expect the unexpected at MAXXI

and where the drivers risk their own and their horses' lives? It's one of cinema's most thrilling scenes! The studios it was filmed in are known as Cinecittà – Hollywood on the River Tiber. The 2010 remake was shot here too when *Boardwalk Empire* actor Jack Huston stepped into the sandals of the late star, Charlton Heston. Internationally famous films like *Quo Vadis*, *Cleopatra* and *Once Upon a Time in the West* were also produced at Cinecittà. Cult film director Federico Fellini, who is responsible for Rome's fame as an international film metropolis and party city with *La Dolce Vita*, even had a flat in the studios. Not much is left of

this cinema mecca, but you can tour the backdrop for Scorsese's *Gangs of New York*, *Romeo and Juliet* and the Roman buildings of the American sketch comedy series *Rome*. Wed-Mon 9.30am–5.30pm | admission 10 euros, with guided tour 20 euros, 2 euros discount on presentation of Metro ticket | cinecittasimostra.it | Metro A Cinecittà | ⌑ 0

⏸ COPPEDÈ QUARTER

Not far from Piazza Buenos Aires a gateway opens onto a stone-built land of fairy tales. This is the strange realm created by Gino Coppedè (1886–1924), inventor of the "Liberty style",

centre. *Daily 7.30am–12.30pm, 4–7.30pm | Largo Terzo Millennio 8–9 | diopadremisericordioso.it | Stazione Termini bus 14 to Quarticcolo | ▢ 0*

59 EUR - ESPOSIZIONE UNIVERSALE DI ROMA

Benito Mussolini had this futuristic quarter built halfway between Rome and Ostia in 1942 for the World's Fair, which never took place thanks to the Second World War. From afar you can see the cuboid *Palazzo della Civiltà del Lavoro* with its 216 window niches. The dome of the *Palazzo dei Congressi* is a pretty perfect example of Fascist architecture, as is the *Museo della Civiltà Romana*, which houses no original works but many excellent copies. The latest architectural addition here is the *La Nuvola* ("the cloud") congress centre. Built by leading architect Massimiliano Fuksas, its outside is simple steel, glass and travertine. Inside a huge "cloud" floats with space for 1,800 guests. Fuksas (who also designed Shenzhen's airport) had to go through decades of bureaucratic wrangling to build his cloud in Rome. *Metro B EUR Palasport | ▢ 0*

> **INSIDER TIP**
> **EUR can do modern too**

> **INSIDER TIP**
> **Disneyland in Stone**

with Art Nouveau palazzi and palatial buildings decorated with figures of fairies, spider-like and fabulous beasts, Babylonian lions' heads and monsters. A decorative frog fountain stands in the *Piazza Mincio* surrounded by dainty *Villini delle fate*, fairies' houses. *Tram 3, 19 | bus 63, 83 | ▢ H4*

58 DIVES IN MISERICORDIA

A must-see for architecture fans: Richard Meier's new steel-and-concrete church in the eastern quarter of *Tor Tre Teste* is about 10km from the

60 MAXXI ★ 🛈

It will take some while for the shock waves triggered by Zaha Hadid's museum for 21st-century art to die down – for both its admirers and its critics. The *Museo Nazionale delle Arti del XXI Secolo*, near the Stadio Flaminio, is an exhibit in itself. Everything is in motion in this building. Ramps suddenly seem to change places as if in a cartoon film, stairs lead up to heaven, and leaning walls or crooked corners tempt visitors to tread new artistic paths at every turn. The collection includes works by artists such as Francesco Clemente, Mario Merz and Gerhard Richter. *Tue–Sun 11am–7pm, Sat 11am–10pm | admission 12 euros | Via Guido Reni 4a | fondazionemaxxi.it | tram 2 | bus 53, 280, 910 | ⏱ 1–2 hrs | ⬚ C2*

🔢 PIGNETO

This trendy suburb has retained a lot of quirky 1950s charm. Jammed in between two arterial roads, Via Prenestina and Via Casilina, this district originally built for railway workers is an area of rented flats, little houses and allotment gardens. Around the main road of the quarter, Via del Pigneto, designers' shops, pubs and literary *enoteche* have sprung up, as Pigneto has attracted lots of musicians, gallery owners, designers, young film-makers and other creative people who can no longer afford the high rents in the Centro Storico. The bar *Necci dal 1924 (Via Fanfulla da Lodi 68)* provided Pier Paolo Pasolini with the right milieu for the pimps and small-time criminals in his film *Accattone*. No other quarter has so many trendy film clubs, such as *Grauco (Via Perugia 34)* and *Cineclub Alphaville (Via del Pigneto 283)*. And nature lovers can take a leafy walk beneath a 2,000-year-old aqueduct, the *Acqua Claudia. Bus 105 | tram 5, 14 | ⬚ M10*

Rome's favourite street food is *porchetta*, served here from a stand in Pigneto

Baths of Caracalla

62 BATHS OF CARACALLA

The romantic ruins of the *Terme di Caracalla* became famous thanks to the first concert it ever held during the 1990 World Cup when the three tenors – Luciano Pavarotti, José Carreras and Plácido Domingo – raised their powerful voices for arias that resounded in the summer night sky, holding the audience spellbound and almost causing the ancient columns to split. Since then, concerts have been held here every summer – now at a safe distance from the decorative and crumbling ruins of the ancient baths where 1,500 people could have wallowed at once. In the summer months, you can enjoy performances here by the *Teatro dell'Opera*. *Mon 9am–1pm, Tue–Sun 9am to one hour before sunset | admission 8 euros | Via delle Terme di Caracalla 52 | Metro B Circo Massimo | bus 628 | 🗺 G12*

TRIPS

CASTELLI ROMANI

25km from Termini, 30 mins by train
The villages and small towns of the *castelli romani*, the roman castles, are situated on what must be the world's oldest wine route. Caesar and Brutus had villas in *Frascati* (about 20km south of Rome) in the Alban Hills. The baroque residence of Cardinal Aldobrandini is not open to visitors, but you can see its park and *Teatro dell'Acqua*. What attracts most day trippers is the delicious white Frascati wine and a portion of suckling pig,

porchetta, eaten at a market stall. *Zaraza (closed Mon, and Sun evening in winter | Viale Regina Margherita 45 | tel. 0 69 42 20 53 | €€)* is a popular place to eat and drink on the beautiful route. On the way to *Castel Gandolfo* you get a wonderful view of a volcanic lake, *Lago di Nemi*, which has lots of good walking trails. The best-known resident of Castel Gandolfo was Pope Benedict XVI. Since 2014, the *Giardino Barberini (guided tours Mon–Sat 8.30 and 11.30am | admission 26 euros | vatican.va)*, the papal park, as well as parts of the summer residence, can be visited by groups (pre-booking required). At the *Hosteria la Fraschetta (closed Mon | Via della Repubblica 58 | tel. 0 69 36 13 12 | €)* you can still get home-made pasta, for example *fettuccine* with porcini mushrooms, for a mere 15 euros. *Directions by train: from Termini to Frascati or Castel Gandolfo; by bus: between Frascati and Castel Gandolfo blue Cotral buses run about every 30 mins. | ▥ 0*

CERVETERI
45km from Termini / 1 hr by car
At a time when Rome was little more than a village, the Etruscan city of *Caere* – now Cerveteri – with its 100,000 inhabitants, was one of the largest cities in the Mediterranean. There are still Etruscan necropolises outside the centre of the modern town. Luckily the *Tomba degli Alari*, the grave of a woman that was discovered in 1905 with a full set of household goods, jewellery and bottles of perfume, escaped millenia of *tombaroli*

(grave robber) activity. Of the eight graves in the *Necropoli di Banditaccia* that are open to visitors, the *Tomba dei Rilievi (Tue–Sun 8.30am–7pm; winter 8.30am–4pm | admission 8 euros)*, aka "tomb of the reliefs" with its stucco decoration, is undoubtedly the most impressive. The grave goods, weapons and religious items found here are on display in the *Museo Nazionale Cerite (Tue–Sun 8.30am–7pm | admission 8 euros, with the Nekropoli 12 euros)* in the *Castello Ruspoli*, a Renaissance palace on Piazza S. Maria in Cerveteri. *Directions by car: Cerveteri, motorway A12 or SS1 Via Aurelia; by train: local train to Ladispoli (towards Grosseto, about 1/hr) from Stazione Termini, change to a blue Cotral bus for Cerveteri, then it's a good 1hr walk to the necropolises; in summer there's a shuttle bus | comune.cerveteri.rm.it | ▥ 0*

TIVOLI

25km from Termini / 1 hr by car

This is a major exhibition on the classical world set among oak, pine and cypress trees. You get to the *Villa Adriana (daily 9am until 1 hr before dusk | admission 8 euros)* just before you arrive in Tivoli, around 30km east of Rome. Obsessed with what he had learned on his travels through the Roman Empire, Emperor Hadrian (76–138 CE) built a palace so he could show his guests some of the Empire's highlights, including the Lyceum and Stoa Poikile, the gate of the Agora in Athens, large and small baths, the valley of temples in Thessaly and the Nile canal between Alexandria and Canopus. The emperor spent downtime in the eccentric Teatro Marittimo, a temple on an island between his philosophers' hall and a Greek and Latin library. Perhaps he was mourning his beautiful young friend Antinous, who died young and whose statues adorn every corner of the residence.

Villa d'Este (Tue–Sun 8.30am until 1 hr before dusk | admission 8 euros | Piazza Villa d'Este 1), in the town of Tivoli, has amazing fountains, which are fed by the *fontana dell'organo idraulico*, a spectacular water feature if ever there was one. Cardinal Ippolito (1509–72) had this terrace-like Renaissance park with its 500 springs and fountains built at the foot of his sumptuous villa. *Directions: take Via Tiburtina, Settecamini to the village of Villa Adriana. By bus: blue Cotral bus from Metro B: Ponte Mammolo to Villa Adriana. It's a 15-min walk to Hadrian's villa, then a short walk to the C.A.T. bus (shuttle) to Tivoli Centro, and 5 mins to Villa d'Este. Return: Cotral bus to Metro B: Ponte Mammolo | comune.tivoli. rm.it |* 📖 0

The Villa d'Este in Tivoli is a popular excursion from the city

EATING & DRINKING

Roman cuisine follows a simple rule: only the best is good enough. Regional, seasonal and fresh ingredients are key: extra virgin olive oil, mind-blowingly tasty tomatoes, dozens of varieties of lettuce and wild vegetables, such as thistles and artichokes – all things the emperors used to eat. Then there are hearty meat dishes like lamb *(abbacchio)* and offal. However, you can skip these and be as veggie as you like here. And then, of course, there is pasta.

Restaurant Gusto

Delis and pasta specialists offer a wider range than most visitors are used to. The pasta alphabet ranges from A for *agnolotti* (meat-filled parcels) and goes to S, the twisted *strozzapreti* (or "priest-stranglers"), or T for *tagliolini* (a kind of ribbon). In Rome, molecular cuisine and fad diets don't stand a chance. "We Romans don't need to follow any trends and fashion because we're legends in our own right," claims Antonello Colonna, Chef at Open Colonna. His restaurant, on the terrace of the Palazzo delle Esposizioni, looks down on the city and on new culinary trends in equal measure.

WHERE ROME EATS

Villa Borghese

Castel S.Angelo

Lungotevere Marzio

📍 Caffetteria Chiostro del Bramante ★

MONTI

The city's hottest bars and coolest ice-cream parlours

📍 Pierluigi ★

📍 Il San Lorenzo ★

Lungotevere dei Tebaldi

Monte Capitolino

Colosseo Ⓜ

Foro Romano

PALATINO

Via dei Cerchi

Lungotevere Aventino

Viale di Trastevere

TESTACCIO

Cucina romana in rustic taverns

Lungotevere Testaccio

Via Marmorata

📍 Checchino dal 1887 ★

Ⓜ Piramide

▲
500 m
547 yd

Via del Porto Fluviale

SALARIO

Via Nomentana

Via Catania

Via XX Settembre

Via Palestro

Viale Regina Elena

Via Tiburtina

SAN LORENZO
Student quarter, with hip bars and a chocolate factory

TIBURTINO

Cimitero di Campo Verano

Via Cavour

Via Giovanni Giolitti

Via dei Ramni

Via Tiburtina

📍 Pommidoro ★

Sciuè Sciuè ★

Cavour

Ⓜ Vittorio Emanuele

Via Merulana

Viale Manzoni

Viale dello Scalo San Lorenzo

Via Labicana

Via Casilina

Via La Spezia

MARCO POLO HIGHLIGHTS

★ **CAFFETTERIA CHIOSTRO DEL BRAMANTE**
Coffee and creativity in the cloister courtyard ➤ p. 82

★ **CHECCHINO DAL 1887**
Dine in the slaughterhouse quarter ➤ p. 86

★ **PIERLUIGI**
Superb grub on the Piazza Ricci with a glass of prosecco as an aperitif to kick things off ➤ p. 87

★ **IL SAN LORENZO**
Fish, fish and more fish around the corner from Campo de' Fiori ➤ p. 87

★ **POMMIDORO**
Trattoria, old-fashioned style with a famous arty clientele ➤ p. 89

★ **SCIUÈ SCIUÈ**
New Roman cuisine served in a pleasant atmosphere ➤ p. 92

Food is still a passion for most Italians – and quality is usually more important than quantity. Breakfast or *colazione*, which is usually enjoyed standing in a bar, is a brief affair, comprising a single *caffè* or a cappuccino and a croissant on the way to the office. These days lunch, or *pranzo*, usually includes a starter *(primo)* and a salad, as people increasingly forego the main course *(secondo)*.

In the evenings at good restaurants it is usual to eat several courses plus *dolce*, a sweet dessert. The best places get booked up so it is a good idea to reserve or get there early (most places open at 7.30pm). When it comes to drinking, Italians usually order a light house wine *(vino sfuso/vino di casa)*, which will be good, cheap and, it goes without saying, dry. A DOC or DOCG sign on the label is a guarantee of the origin by region or location. White wines made nearby in Castelli Romani, e.g. Frascati, are popular, as are the refreshing Orvieto, Vernaccia di San Gimignano and dry Verdicchio. Restaurant owners will give you a funny look if you just order beer but no food. If you are not hungry but want a drink, hunt out a *vinoteca*, or wine bar.

Italians make a little ritual out of paying for a meal. The waiter brings the bill *(il conto)* – 15 per cent service is usually included – and brings back exact change down to the last cent. If you were satisfied, you leave up to five per cent on the plate. Unfortunately, standards of service and courtesy have fallen noticeably in recent years, especially in the touristy areas. Make sure you ask for an official bill *(ricevuta fiscale)*, as tax inspectors sometimes make checks.

CAFÉS & GELATERIE

If you just want a *caffè* or a juice, order it at the bar. Table service can cost you up to three times as much, particularly in touristy spots.

ATELIER CANOVA TADOLINI ☂

In what was once the studio of the sculptor and architect Antonio Canova you can either enjoy your cappuccino or aperitif at the bar or in an expensive armchair surrounded by works in plaster and marble and pretend to be an artist for a few minutes. Unfortunately, the sculptures are copies. Even a trip to the WC and its crazy door is full of surprises. This is a popular meeting spot near the Spanish Steps. *Daily 8am–midnight | Via del Babuino 150 | canovatadolini.com | Metro A Spagna | Centro | ⊞ E6*

CAFFETTERIA CHIOSTRO DEL BRAMANTE ★

On a terrace above the elegant Renaissance courtyard built by Bramante you can enjoy coffee or brunch (Sun from 11am), have an aperitif from 5pm, browse in the bookshop or view an exhibition. From the *Sala delle Sibille* on the first floor you can also catch a glimpse of Raphael's frescoes of the Sibyls in the neighbouring church of *Santa Maria della Pace* (see p. 46). Doubly good as the church is seldom open. *Mon–Fri 10am–8pm, Sat/Sun 10am–9pm | Arco*

Be inspired by the sculptures in Café-Atelier Canova Tadolini

della Pace 5 | chiostrodelbramante.it | bus 40, 62, 64 | *Centro* | 🚇 D8

CAMBIOVITA

The name of this small café says it all: CamBIOvita! Everything is organic and either vegetarian or vegan. *Daily 8am–11pm | Via del Governo Vecchio 54/44 | bus 40, 60, 62, 64 | Centro | 🚇 D8*

I DOLCI DI CHECCO ER CARRETTIERE

There are very few horse-drawn carriages *(carretiere)* left in Rome but this horsey *osteria* has managed to maintain a distinctly Roman charm for three generations. A few years ago the current owners took over the café next door. A blessing for us all as they have turned it into the best ice-cream shop in Trastevere. Make sure you try the pistachio! *Daily 12.30–3pm, 7.30–10pm | Via Benedetta 10 | bus H, tram 8 | Trastevere | 🚇 D9*

GELATERIA GIOLITTI 🚩

Rome's most famous ice-cream salon has been in business since 1900 and half of Parliament are regulars. The selection is huge. Traditionalists order the *bacio* chocolate ice cream or the truffle ice cream. Fruit sorbets, champagne flavour and ginger are also chart-toppers here. Very near the Pantheon and Parliament. *Daily 7–2am | Via Uffici del Vicario 40 | giolitti.it | bus 62, 63 | Centro | 🚇 E8*

> **INSIDER TIP**
> **Ice cream for the elite**

GINGER

In this organic bistro and café situated on the exclusive Via Borgognona, health-conscious Romans sip their smoothies, organic fruit juices, herbal teas and even a good old cappuccino from time to time. *Daily 10am–midnight | Via Borgognona 43–44 | bus 62, 63 | Metro A Spagna | Centro | ⧜ E7*

GREZZO RAW CHOCOLATE

Raw chocolate – the sweetest-sounding organic product ever? The people in the queue on the Via Urbana certainly think so. From ice cream and chocolates to truffles and cakes, everything in the store is made from raw chocolate. The unprocessed cocoa contains all the original nutrients and is a rich source of anti-oxidants. Ice cream without the guilty conscience! *Daily 11am–11pm | Via Urbana 130 | grezzoitalia.it | Metro B Cavour | Monti | ⧜ G6*

> **INSIDER TIP**
> Eat more chocolate!

GROM

Two young Turinese with the perfect idea for ice cream. They grow their own organic fruit on their farms in Piedmont and turn it into a super-*gelato*. Top tip: try the cantaloupe melon! They also have branches near the Pantheon *(Via della Maddalena 30)* and in the Stazione Termini. *Sun–Thu 11–1am, Fri/Sat 11–1.30am | Piazza Navona 1 | bus 40, 64, 70, 81, 492 | Centro | ⧜ D8*

SAID–ANTICA FABBRICA DEL CIOCCOLATO ☂

In this old San Lorenzo chocolate factory dating from 1923 you can sample the chocolatiers' creations (the ricotta-filled pralines are to die for). Sit in the café on trendy barstools made of old milk churns and order a hot chocolate: the milk will be well frothed and the spoon will stand upright. The chefs ensure chocolate features across the menu. *Tue–Sun 10–1am | Via Tiburtina 135/ Via Marrucini | tel. 0 64 46 92 04 | said.it | tram/bus 3, 19 | San Lorenzo | ⧜ K8*

> **INSIDER TIP**
> A lot of chocolate

SANT'EUSTACHIO

The aroma emanating from Rome's oldest coffee roasters wafts over Piazza Sant'Eustachio, where other *cafés* have set up shop. The caffè comes already sweetened unless you order it *"senza zucchero"*. The baristas are less sweet and need some warming up if you want to get a smile out of them. *Daily 8.30–1am | Piazza Sant'Eustachio 82 | bus 75 | Centro | ⧜ E8*

SCIASCIA CAFFÈ

You can easily miss this historic café dating from 1919. It has no tables outside but inside it looks like an elegant Belle Époque Viennese coffee house. The green upholstered armchairs, vintage sofa and panelled walls are inviting, and the cappuccino – one of the best in Rome is served in small porcelain cups by Riccardo Ginori. The café, which is a favourite with young lawyers, doctors and legal

Today's Specials

Antipasti

CARCIOFI ALLA GIUDIA
Crispy artichokes fried in olive oil

PANZANELLA
A summery salad of white bread with tomatoes, olive oil and basil

CAPRESE DI BUFALA E POMODORO
Buffalo mozzarella, tomatoes and basil

Pasta

ORECHIETTE AL BROCCOLO
Ear-shaped pasta with broccoli and prawns

BUCATINI ALL'AMATRICIANA
Pasta with a tomato and bacon sauce and pecorino cheese

PASTA E FAGIOLI
A soup of beans and tube-shaped pasta

TONNARELLI, CACIO E PEPE
Chunky spaghetti with a creamy cheese and pepper sauce

Secondi

CONIGLIO ALLA CACCIATORA
Roasted rabbit with rosemary

SALTIMBOCCA ALLA ROMANA
Veal or turkey schnitzel with sage and parma ham

TAGLIATA DI MANZO, RUCOLA, GRANA E POMODORI
Sliced steak with rocket, tomatoes and grana cheese

POLLO ALLA ROMANA CON PEPERONI E PATATE
Fried chicken with peppers and sautéed potatoes

ABBACCHIO ALLA SCOTTADITO
Lamb chops with roast potatoes

Dolci

CANNOLO
Sweet pastry rolls from Sicily, made famous by *The Godfather II*

PANNA COTTA CON FRAGOLE
A set vanilla custard with strawberries

With three Michelin stars, Heinz Beck's La Pergola is a culinary highlight of Rome

clerks, is situated in the Prati quarter near the Vatican. *Daily 7am–8pm | Via Fabio Via Massimo 80 | sciascia1919. com | Metro A Ottaviano/San Pietro or Lepanto | Monti | Ⅲ C6*

RESTAURANTS €€€

ANTONELLO COLONNA – OPEN BISTRO

The décor in this gourmet restaurant on the rooftop terrace of the Palazzo delle Esposizioni is cool and modern. Try the *tortelli* with duck liver pâté, *cappeletti* with prawns, squid with potatoes or pigeon with polenta. Incidentally, the Open Colonna is not a one-trick pony: at lunchtime, you can sample the *City Lunch (Tue–Sat 12.30pm–3.30pm)*, a superb vegetarian buffet for 16 euros, while at weekends brunch is popular *(Sat/Sun 12.30–3.30pm | 30 euros/pers)* with large Roman families coming out to dine. *Gourmet restaurant: Tue–Sat from 7pm reservation only | Via Milano 9a | tel. 06 47 82 26 41 | antonellocolonna.it | bus 64, 70, 170 | Trevi | Ⅲ G8*

CHECCHINO DAL 1887 ★

This upmarket trattoria, which serves hearty Roman food, attracts a high-ranking international clientele, including lots of famous politicians. Its specialities all include offal, thanks to its location next to the old abattoir. The wine list is excellent. *Tue–Sat | Via Monte Testaccio 30 | tel. 0 65 74 38 16 | checchino-dal-1887. com | bus 170 | Testaccio | Ⅲ D12*

LA PERGOLA

Well, he is the King of Rome, after all: Heinz VIII as the Romans affectionately call him! Heinz Beck, who was voted top chef for the first time in 1997, has maintained three Michelin stars for several years. The nine-course menu on the rooftop terrace of the luxury hotel Cavalieri Waldorf Astoria with views of Rome and celebrities is a snip at 220 euros. *Tue–Sat evenings only | Via Alberto Cadlolo 101 | tel. 0 63 50 91 | romecavalieri.it | bus 907, 913 | Trionfale | A3*

PIERLUIGI ★

With a great location on the romantic Piazza dei Ricci, you can watch Rome's great and good go by while you tuck into delicious food. The fish, spaghetti with langoustine sauce, carpaccio and chocolate cake are famous locally – as are the prices. Try the dry house Prosecco, Bernabei, for a bit of sparkle with your meal. Rather expensive. *Tue–Sun | Piazza de' Ricci 144 | tel. 0 66 86 87 17 | tel. 0 66 86 13 02 | bus 64 | Centro | C–D 8–9*

IL SAN LORENZO ★

Fish does not all taste the same. The San Lorenzo restaurant near the Campo de'Fiori serves the finest tuna, bream, sea urchins and langoustine carpaccio. Excellent wine list, with prices to match. *Mon–Sat | Via dei Chiavari 4 | tel. 0 66 86 50 97 | ilsan lorenzo.it | bus 40, 62, 64, 116 | Centro | D9*

LE VOLTE

This *ristorante* is a godsend for all those who love classic Mediterranean food without too much fuss. Despite its central location on the small Piazza Rondanini near the Pantheon, it is well hidden. Whether you order the *insalata del mare, saltimbocca* (with

veal – as it is in all the best places) or the *tonnarelli alla pescatora,* the chef, Pietro, knows what his guests are after. Even the Chief of Police is a regular here. *Thu–Tue 12–3pm and 7pm–midnight | Piazza Rondanini 47 | tel. 0 66 87 74 08 | levolte.thefork.rest | bus 40, 62, 64 | Centro | E7*

RESTAURANTS €€

ANTICA HOSTARIA L'ARCHEOLOGIA

If you are looking for a good restaurant with a nice garden to wind down after a dusty walk on Via Appia Antica, this is it. Wisteria and roses bloom, little fountains gurgle and the pasta dishes, e.g. with fish and mussels, are just lip-smackingly superb. *Daily | Via Appia Antica 139 | tel. 0 67 88 04 94 | bus 118 | K–L16*

AROMATICUS GREEN BAR

This small restaurant is almost drowning in greenery. Pretty flowers and a selection of vegetable and herbs grow out of every corner. Their sensational scent may well have you reaching for your wallet – they are all available to buy and take home. The owners, Luca and Francesca, are members of the urban gardening movement as their stunning roof terrace will prove. Try their quirky takes on sustainable eating with dishes like soup, beef tartare and carpaccio available for as little as 10 euros. They also do takeaway. *Tue–Sun 10am–9pm | Via Urbana 134 | tel. 0 64 88 13 55 | aromaticus.it | Metro B Cavour | Monti | G8*

EATALY

A paradise for gluttons spread over two floors, where you can choose from a range of 23 slow-food restaurants and stands as well as stock up on the finest olive oils, organic wines, hundreds of different types of pasta and cookbooks. *Daily 10am–midnight | ex-air terminal Ostiense | Piazzale 12 Octobre 1492 | roma.eataly.it | bus 60, 95, 121, 175, 280 Piazzale di Partigiani (badly signposted) | Metro B Piramide (300m through an underpass to Stazione Ostiense) | Ostiense | ⑪ F13–14*

DA FELICE

Da Felice is always packed and very hospitable. The restaurateur apparently serves the city's best *spaghetti carbonara* or *tonnarelli cacio e pepe*. Their famous slogan is, "Our dishes have stayed the same since 1936". Some Romans feel they have won the lottery if they land a table at this eatery (reservation by phone only). *Daily | Via Mastro Giorgio 29/Via Galvani | tel. 0 65 74 68 00 | feliceatestaccio.it | Metro B Piramide | bus 83, 121, 673 | Testaccio | ⑪ E12*

FLAVIO AL VELAVEVODETTO

If you enjoy eating kidneys, liver and intestines, this is the place for you. The owner can barely spell the word "vegan" let alone cook for one. If the waiters' brash humour is likely to get on your nerves after a long day or you'd rather avoid the crowds around the Testaccio, you can always have lunch there instead of dinner. In the day you will probably get a table in the rusty red courtyard. But if you want to do what the Romans do and have a fun evening munching on meat, make sure to dine there (reservation is a must). *Daily 12.30–11pm | Via di Monte Testaccio 97 | tel. 0 65 74 41 94 | Metro B Piramide | bus 83, 121, 673 | Testaccio | ⑪ E12*

GINA

Gina's is actually a high-class snack bar serving sandwiches of salmon, beef and swordfish carpaccio. But the real sensation here is Gina's picnic basket to take away to the nearby Villa Borghese Park: posh sandwiches, wine (or prosecco if you'd prefer), cheese, fresh fruit, home-made pastries, espresso in a thermos, corkscrew and tablecloth (approx. 45–65 euros). *Via San Sebastiano 7a | Piazza di Spagna | tel. 0 66 78 02 51 | gina roma.com | Metro A Spagna | Centro | ⑪ E7*

NUOVO MERCATO DI TESTACCIO

This market built out of glass and concrete opened in 2012. In Rome that makes it brand new but the cool mix of old-school stalls, trendy pasta chefs and Roman street food (spelt "strit fut"), often

experimenting with popular dishes such as tiramisu, has quickly established it as a firm favourite. Everything looks amazing too.

In Danilo Mastroianni's bar the actor Marcello grins down from the wall. He's Danilo's uncle, apparently. The queue outside Mordi e Vai (English: "Eat up and get out") is always impressive as people hanker after their meaty sandwiches – some of which contain traditional Roman offal. Allesandra and Allessandro make the best pasta in this district in their Laboratorio Le Mani in Pasta. Tuck in! *Daily 6am-3pm | Via Galvani Metro B Piramide | tram 3 | bus 83, 121, 673 | Testaccio | ▥ D12*

PEPPO AL COSIMATO

Everyone can put surf 'n' turf together. Franky's cunning trick is to put fish into Italy's national dish: pizza. A true local favourite in the district – no stodgy dough here. Instead, it is beautifully crisp with delicious local ingredients including *mozzarella di bufala* from Pontina (south of Rome). Franky and his team have a talent for fish. Get the *supplis* (rice balls) for your starter, either *al nero* (in a squid ink sauce) or the *supplis a ragu di mare* (with a seafood ragu). The *taglioni* with seafood tartare are superb. If you don't like fish, stick to a traditional pizza. *Daily 12-3pm and 6pm-midnight | Via Natale del Grande 10 | tel. 0 65 81 20 48 | tram 8 | bus H | Trastevere | ▥ D10*

POMMIDORO ★

The *letterati* Alberto Moravia and Pier Paolo Pasolini philosophised here over their *spaghetti all'amatriciana*. The landlord never cashed Pasolini's last cheque, which he wrote the

Parmigiano Reggiano for sale in Eataly's food court

Pommidoro: this old-school Italian trattoria attracts writers and artists

evening before he died. The artists, glitterati, and eccentric characters of San Lorenzo still meet here because Anna and Aldo's food is so good. *Mon–Sat | Piazza dei Sanniti 44 | tel. 0 64 45 26 92 | tram/bus 3, 19 | ⌘ K8*

PORTO FLUVIALE

This beautiful old warehouse is the new place to be seen in Testaccio/Ostiense. Trattoria, birreria, BBQ, buffet, pub and cocktail bar all in one. *Mon–Fri large lunchtime buffet for 10 euros. Daily 10.30am–2pm | Via Porto Fluviale 22 | portofluviale.com | Metro B Piramide | bus 23, 83, 271, 673 | ⌘ E13*

IL TAVOLO, IL VINO E LA DISPENSA

Up for dinner in a station café? It may not sound great but two-star chef Oliver Glowig has been dishing out food in this station for two years. And it is superb. Fortunately, his prices have recently dropped, so now no main course costs more than 20 euros. Try the juicy *tonno spada* or Glowig's signature dish, *eliche, cacio, pepe e ricci di mare* (pasta with cheese and fresh sea urchins). The restaurant also sells wine, cheese and top-quality ingredients. *Daily 12 noon–9pm | Mercato Centrale in Termini Station | entrance on Via Giolitti 36 | tel. 06 46 20 29 89 | oliverglowig.com | Metro A, B Termini | Esquilino | ⌘ H8–9*

INSIDER TIP
Best station restaurant anywhere

RESTAURANTS €

ANTICA OSTERIA DA GIOVANNI

You need to get to this simple old *osteria* early because it is popular with everyone, from rich local residents to busy builders. The pasta is home-made (of course) and wine is all by the glass. Good value for money. *Mon–Sat | Via della Lungara 41a | tel. 0 66 86 15 14 | bus 23, 280 | Trastevere | ⊞ C9*

DA AUGUSTO ▶

A good, old-fashioned Trastevere trattoria. You sit out on the *piazza* and more often than not Augusto, the host, will personally lay the paper table-cloth and immediately take your order. If you can't understand his accent, simply order the dish of the day from the blackboard, e.g. *coniglio* (rabbit) or *pollo* (chicken). *Closed Sat evenings and Sun | Piazza de' Renzi 15 | tel. 0 65 80 37 98 | tram 8 | Trastevere | ⊞ D10*

IL BOCCONCINO

Just behind the Colosseum, Nelly and Giancarlo – who is actually a pharmacist – have opened a slow-food trattoria that has become a real hit in the local area. Try their traditional Roman-style starters such as *polpette di melanzane e pinoli* (aubergine dumplings with pine kernels), *crostini di alici* (toast with anchovies) or *spezzatino di vitella* (veal stew with beans). *Thu–Tue | Via Ostilia 23 | tel. 06 77 07 91 75 | Metro B Colosseo | bus 75, 81, 85, 117 | tram 3 | Monti | ⊞ G10*

ENZO AL 29

The tiny trattoria tucked away in a small alley in Trastevere has just a few wobbly tables outside on the cobblestones. If you're lucky enough to have a reserved table for the evening, you should arrive promptly. After ten minutes, Enzo gives the table to the next in line. Meanwhile, Enzo, Giulia and Francesco serve all those waiting with a glass of wine. Their reputation is well-earned: try the lasagne with pine nuts, pumpkin flowers stuffed with mozzarella and anchovies or *rigatoni alla matriciana*. *Tue–Sun 12.30–3pm and 7.30–10pm | Via dei Vascellari 29/ Via dei Genovesi | tel. 0 65 81 22 60 | daenzoal29.com | tram 8 | Trastevere | ⊞ E10*

DA FRANCO AR VICOLETTO

For 30 years Franco's regulars in the university and workers' quarter of San Lorenzo have been coming here – originally as students, now accompanied by their children. A three-course menu costs 30 euros, starter and main course for 20 euros. *Tue–Sun | Via dei Falisci 3 | tel. 0 64 95 76 75 | bus 71 | San Lorenzo | ⊞ K8*

HOSTARIA ROMANESCA

Come for the view alone! This is a place to experience life's sunny side – on the buzzing, vibrant Campo de' Fiori. The cooking is basic but good with plain Roman dishes like *spaghetti carbonara* and *pollo ai peperoni*. Book a table! *Daily | Campo de' Fiori 40 | tel. 0 66 86 20 24 | bus 40, 62| Parione/Centro | ⊞ D9*

SCIUÈ SCIUÈ ★

Francesco creates a new menu every day with fresh vegetables, fish and pasta at this attractive informal restaurant in Monti. Dishes include baked courgette flowers or tuna tartare with oranges and pine nuts, and prices are affordable. *Daily | Via Urbana 56–57 | tel. 06 48 90 60 38 | sciuesciueroma. com | Metro B Cavour | | Monti | ⊞ G9*

SERGIO ALLE GROTTE

This wonderfully old-fashioned trattoria is hidden away in an alley off Via Giubbonari behind Campo de' Fiori. The food is every bit as 1950s as the red and white checked tablecloths. Try Sergio's take on classics such as spaghetti amatriciana or puttanesca. There's fresh fish on Tue, Fri and Sat. *Mon–Sat | Vicolo delle Grotte 27 | tel. 06 86 42 93 | tram 8 | bus 30, 40, 62, 63, 64 | ⊞ D9*

INSIDER TIP
Picture-postcard trattoria

TRAM TRAM

The name derives from the tram that trundles by on its way to Porta Maggiore. The cooking is Roman with Sicilian and Pugliese influences e.g. *orechiette alla Norma* (ear-shaped pasta with vegetables), *rigatoni alla pajatina* (with calf's intestines) and *gnocchi con baccalà*, (with cod). *Tue–Sun | Via dei Reti 46 | tel. 06 49 04 16 | tramtram.it | tram 3, 19 | bus 492 | San Lorenzo | ⊞ L8*

BUCCONE

Where horses were once stabled, exquisite wines are stored today. Enjoy them with light dishes such as pasta and baked aubergine, and an array of high-quality olive oils and balsamic vinegars. *Mon–Thu lunch only, Fri/Sat evenings too | Via di Ripetta 19–20 | tel. 0 63 61 21 54 | enoteca buccone.com | Metro A Flaminio | Centro | ⊞ E6*

VINI, VIZI E VIRTÙ

"Wines, vices and virtues" is the name of this small, charming wine bar just five minutes away from the Vatican, where Antonio Mazzitelli recommends excellent wines to his guests at decent prices. It's a popular spot for young Romans. *Mon–Sat | Piazza dell'Unità 15 | tel. 06 89 53 70 95 | Metro A Ottaviano-San Pietro | tram 19 | bus 81 | Prati | ⊞ B–C6*

VINOROMA

With her themed Italian wine tastings, the sommelière Hande Leimer has created an iconic Roman experience, guiding you through seven Italian wines in her pretty flat in the old town (50 euros/person). *Daily by prior arrangement | Via in Selci 84/G | tel. 32 84 87 44 97 | vinoroma.com | bus C3, 84, 75 | Metro B Cavour | Monti | ⊞ G9*

PIZZERIAS & TAVOLE CALDE

ALLE FRATTE DI TRASTEVERE

Good crispy pizzas, simple Roman cuisine and friendly service. Situated at the heart of the trendy district of Trastevere, this old pizzeria has long been a solid good-value option. *Thu–Tue | Via delle Fratte di Trastevere 49–50 | next to Ospedale San Gallicano | tel. 0 65 83 57 75 | tram H, 8 | Trastevere | ᗕ D10*

DA BAFFETTO

An established institution close to Piazza Navona. Hungry customers queue here every evening. *Daily, evenings only | Via del Governo Vecchio 114 | tel. 0 66 86 16 17 | bus 40, 62, 64 | ᗕ D8*

IL BOSCAIOLO

Pizzeria north of the Trevi Fountain with a wide selection of toppings and thin, crispy dough. The salads are good, too. *Tue–Sun | Via degli Artisti 37 | tel. 0 64 88 40 23 | Metro A Barberini Centro | ᗕ F7*

ER BUCHETTO

Three plain wooden tables and no choice at all: what Franco makes is genuine *porchetta*, a Roman pork dish seasoned with salt, pepper and fennel. The juicy roast is cooked on a rotating spit and eaten with white bread. From 5 euros per portion. *Mon–Sat 10am–3pm, 5–9pm | Via del Viminale 2f | Metro A/B B Termini Cavour | bus 40, 64 | Esquilino | ᗕ G–H8*

Hostaria Romanesca serves up typical Roman fare on Campo de' Fiori

SHOPPING

Alta moda in the palazzi, funky crafts and vintage finds in the small side streets – Italian design is unrivalled and there's no shortage in Rome.

The A to Z of fashion goes from Armani to Zegna, the greying doyenne designers whose boutiques are housed in chic inner-city palazzi. The Piazza di Spagna looks like the centrefold of *Vogue* magazine with Gucci, Prada, Versace, Dolce & Gabbana and the jeweller Bulgari. The Via Condotti and Via Borgognona tempt a global clientele with big pockets to indulge in expensive sprees.

Window display for Valentino

The elegant shopping "gallery" on the corner of the Via del Corso/Via del Tritone – ☂ *Galleria Alberto Sordi* – is surely worth a glance.

Monti is an excellent area for fans of vintage and bargains. You will also find retro and second-hand stores in the Via del Governo Vecchio or the Via dei Banchi Nuovi near the Tiber. Small shops around the Pantheon and the Campo de' Fiori sell handmade leather items in any design you can imagine.

WHERE ROME SHOPS

CITTÀ DEL VATICANO

Castel S. Angelo

San Pietro

Lungotevere Marzio

Aldo Fefe ⭐ 📍

Via di Porta Cavalleggeri

Lungotevere Gianicolense

Corso Vittorio Emanuele II

Ibiz Artigianato di Cuoio ⭐ 📍

Tevere

Pandora della Malva ⭐ 📍

AURELIO

TRASTEVERE

Stationers and gift shops, small boutiques and colourful markets

Villa Doria Pamphili

Via Giacinto Carini

Viale di Trastevere

400 m
437 yd

Porta Portese ⭐ 📍

MARCO POLO HIGHLIGHTS

⭐ **CUCINELLI**
Finest cashmere, exclusive prices, social conscience: Brunello Cucinelli ➤ p. 100

⭐ **GUCCI**
Luxury-brand accessories and bags large and small ➤ p. 101

⭐ **IBIZ ARTIGIANATO DI CUOIO**
Handmade handbags in every colour imaginable ➤ p. 101

⭐ **SERMONETA GLOVES**
The best place to buy elegant Italian leather gloves ➤ p. 102

Villa Borghese

SALARIO

Ⓜ Spagna

📍 **Gucci** ★
📍 **Sermoneta Gloves** ★
📍 **Cucinelli** ★

AROUND THE SPANISH STEPS

High fashion and flagship stores, from Armani to Zegna

Barberini Ⓜ

Via del Quirinale

Via Nazionale

Via Cernaia

Via Marsala

Via Giovanni Giolitti

Via Cavour

Ⓜ Cavour

MONTI

Designer boutiques, plus second-hand and vintage shops

Via dei Fori Imperiali

Monte Capitolino

Colosseo Ⓜ

Foro Romano

Colosseo

PALATINO

Via dei Cerchi

Via del Circo Massimo

Via di San Gregorio

Via dell'Amba Aradam

Circo Massimo Ⓜ

★ **ALDO FEFE**
Old-style stationer and bookbinder ➤ p. 104

★ **PANDORA DELLA MALVA**
1,000 great gifts, from necklaces to clutch bags and lamps ➤ p. 105

★ **PORTA PORTESE**
Sunday flea market in Trastevere – a genuine Roman institution ➤ p. 106

Roman's oldest herbalist: Antica Erboristeria Romana

Don't forget, Rome is great place to shop for food as well as fashion. Markets like Piazza San Cosimato or the numerous small *alimentari* (delicatessens) offer appetizing souvenirs to take back home such as Parmigiano, olive oil or Parma ham.

Many shops are open from 10am to 8pm, but some close between 1pm and 4 or 5pm in the summer heat. In winter everything stays closed on Monday morning – except the food shops.

WHERE TO START?

The bus stop on **Largo Chigi/ Piazza San Silvestro** (*▢▢ E7*), where the pedestrianised area begins, is a good starting point for shopping spree. From here you are within easy reach of the exclusive boutiques in the area between Via Frattina, Via Condotti and Via Borgognona and Piazza di Spagna, but you can also stroll along the much cheaper Via del Corso. *Metro A Spagna | bus 52, 53, 61, 62, 63, 71, 80, 85, 95, 492*

BOOKSHOPS

FELTRINELLI

The German photographer, Inge Feltrinelli, took portraits of some of the most famous people in the world – the likes of Garbo, Hemingway, JFK and Picasso – before she married the publisher Giangiacomo Feltrinelli. The Milan-based publisher has three modern bookshops and an excellent range of international literature. *Galleria Alberto Sordi 33 | Metro A Spagna | Centro | ⊞ E8; Via E. Orlando 84 | Metro A Repubblica | Centro | ⊞ G7; also Sun 10am–9pm | Largo di Torre Argentina 11 | bus 62, 64 | Centro | ⊞ E9*

OPEN DOOR BOOKSHOP

International bookstores are gradually becoming hard to find, and Rome now only has a handful of them. But this welcoming shop in Trastevere has been going for 40 years. It mostly stocks second-hand books in Italian, English, German and Spanish. *Via della Lungaretta 23 | books-in-italy. com | tram 8 | bus H | Trastevere | ⊞ E10*

DESIGN & DÉCOR

ARTEMIDE

From Tolomeo table lamps to silver Alfiere hanging lights and Arcadia bedside lamps – at Artemide's they are switched on to all the latest trends. *Via Margutta 107 | artemide.com | Metro A Spagna | Centro | ⊞ E6*

BOSCHETTO TRE

Mobiles with butterflies, dragonfly magnets, dog face cushions, stylish light bulbs, and rugs made of recycled materials: the designer Oriana Tombolesi splendidly combines all kinds of materials. *Via Boschetto 3 | boschettotre.it | Metro A Spagna | Monti | ⊞ G8*

FRATELLI PINCI

A lion's head or a lamp fitting – this wonderful old-fashioned shop is as stuffed as a Middle Eastern bazaar. The Pinci brothers have thousands of classical brass objets d'art and water taps. You just need a palace to put them in… *Via del Babuino 128 | Metro A Spagna | Centro | ⊞ E6*

MAURIZIO GROSSI

The Venus de Milo, a bust of Caesar or an obelisk for your living room? Copies of ancient art as modern design objects. *Via Margutta 109 | mauriziogrossi.com | Metro A Spagna | Centro | ⊞ E6*

NORA P

A stylish bathtub filled with flowering orchids or colourful deckchairs to brighten up your front room? Nora Pastore's designs are *avant garde* even in trendy Monti. *Via Panisperna 220–221 | nora-p.com | Metro B Cavour | bus 117 | Monti | ⊞ G8*

FASHION

ARMANI

His career plan was originally to become a surgeon, but then Giorgio Armani decided to operate in the world of fashion. His creations, from suits to the trendy Emporio line, perfumes and lifestyle products, are synonymous with Italian good taste. And the king of business fashion – non-crease, timeless, no wear and tear– still rules the roost in his flagship store close to the Spanish Steps. *Via Condotti 77 | armani.com | Metro A Spagna | Centro | ⊞ E7*

ARSENALE

Cutting-edge but not all that expensive. Designer fashion by Patrizia Pieroni. And you can purchase fun artworks here too. *Via del Pellegrino 172 | patriziapieroni.it | bus 40, 62, 64 | Centro | ⬚ D8*

BORSALINO

A 150-year-old hat worn by gangsters, gigolos and gentlemen. If you want to buy the wide-brimmed real deal, you needed to start saving a while ago … *Piazza del Popolo 20 | borsalino.com | bus 117, 119 | Centro | ⬚ E6; also Via di Campo Marzio 72a | bus 62, 63 | Centro | ⬚ E7*

CASTEL ROMANO OUTLET

You can get large discounts on luxury brands such as Trussardi, Ferré, Zegna, Loro Piano, Burberry, Lacoste and Calvin at the Castel Romano outlet on the Via Pontina, around 25km south of the city centre. *Mon–Thu 10am–8pm, Fri–Sun 10am–9pm | Via Ponte di Piscina Cupa 64 | Castel Romano | shuttle bus from Via Marsala 71 (Stazione Termini) | departures 9.30am, 9.55am, 11.30am, 12.30pm, 3pm, return 11.20am, 1.45pm, 5.15pm and 8.05pm | 15 euros | outlet-village.it/castelromano | Castel Romano/Pontina | ⬚ 0*

CUCINELLI ★

Umbrian Brunello Cucinelli is not only famous for his cashmere hoodies but also for his social conscience. His factory is a former country estate in the enchanting village of Solomeo, which he has completely restored. This style has rubbed off on his boutique in Via Borgognona. But the prices are *prezzi alle stelle* – sky high! *Via Borgognona 33 | bus 52, 53, 61, 62, 80, 83*

EDO CITY

In Monti, fashion designer Alessandra Giannetti (an ex-resident of London and Tokyo) turns out suits for women, linen raincoats and casual trousers in beautiful pastel colours in her very own Japanese-Italian style. *Via Leonina 78–79 | alessandragiannetti.com | Metro B Cavour | Centro | ⬚ E8*

FENDI

The five Fendi sisters rule over a Roman empire of furs, fashion and cosmetics (today belonging to the French luxury giant LVMH) with a showroom in a glass palazzo on the Corso. Ilaria Venturini Fendi, a granddaughter of the founders, left the business in 2006 to set up her own recycled brand "Carmina Campus", which sells its wares in the *Re(fuse)* boutique *(Via Fontanella Borghese 40)* a few doors down from Fendi's temple to luxury. *Largo Carlo Goldoni 36–40 | fendi.com | Metro A Spagna | Centro | ⬚ E7*

FURLA

In 1955 Aldo and Margherita sold their first solid but elegant leather bags designed for strong, independent women. The upmarket bag producers from Bologna have recently adopted a hipper look and moved over to other materials. They have shops everywhere, including on Rome's most exclusive shopping

Paper is his passion: Aldo Fefe is a master bookbinder

street. *Via Condotti 55–56 | furla.com | bus 61, 62, 63 | Metro A Spagna | Centro | ☐ E7*

LE GALLINELLE
Exciting ways of breathing new life into old objects: in Monti, Wilma Silvestri recycles fabrics and transforms them into fantastic fashion. *Via Panisperna 60 | Metro B Cavour | ☐ G8*

GUCCI ★
World-famous and pretty posh: leather bags and exclusive fashion accessories by this luxury brand. *Via Condotti 8 | gucci.com | Metro A Spagna | Centro | ☐ E7*

IBIZ ARTIGIANATO DI CUOIO ★
A chic, handmade leather clutch bag or garish purse? Since 1972, the Nepi family has made handcrafted leather goods at surprisingly reasonable prices. You can glimpse how the new pieces are made in the workshop at the back. Loyal customers from around the world send Elisa Nepi selfies with their new handbags. *Via dei Chiavari 39 | Centro | ☐ D9*

MASSIMO DUTTI
Sleek style for men which the women's collection can't quite match. *Via del Corso 14–16 | Galleria Alberto Sordi | massimodutti.com | bus 62, 63, 116, 117, 119 | Centro | ☐ E8*

MAX MARA
Smart rags from an Italian designer, who founded a fashion empire from his parents' small dressmaker's shop. *Via Condotti 17–19 and Via Frattina 28 | Metro A Spagna | Centro | ☐ E7*

NUYORICA

Celebs like Cameron Diaz do their shopping here. A T-shirt will cost a month's salary but it's fun to look inside, and that's free. *Piazza Pollarola 36–37 | bus 40, 63, 116 | Centro | ▥ D9*

RINASCENTE

In order to create this luxurious lair on the shabby Via del Tritone, a small fortune had to be invested. The department store's new flagship shop has an ideal location on the tourist mile between the Trevi Fountain and the Spanish Steps but it lacks the class of the high-end boutiques on the Via Borgognoni and Via Condotti.

INSIDER TIP
Café on an aqueduct

The best thing about it is the view over Rome from the champagne bar on the roof and the 60-m Roman aqueduct in the cellar (which has its own café/bar and light shows). *Via del Tritone 61 | rinascente.it | bus 62, 63, 83, 85, 160, 492 | Metro A Barberini-Fontana di Trevi | Trevi/Centro | ▥ F7*

SERMONETA GLOVES ★

Leather gloves? Out of fashion for a long while, they are back in again. Giorgio Sermoneta Senior always believed in the return of this elegant item – and he now heads a glove emporium with stores in Milan, Venice and New York. His favourite shop is at the Spanish Steps in Rome. *Piazza di Spagna 61 | Metro A Spagna | Centro | ▥ F7*

TALARICO

This traditional Neapolitan tailor makes the top-end ties and cravats that Berlusconi and Bill Clinton wear. *Via dei Coronari 51 | bus 40, 62, 64 | Centro | ▥ D8*

LA SELLA

Fashionable leather bags, purses, wallets and belts, all at affordable prices. *Via della Cuccagna/Piazza Navona | bus 40, 46, 62, 64 | Centro | ▥ D8*

VALENTINO

One of the last grand aristocrats of the fashion business, who helped to invent *dolce vita* culture and whose togs have adorned many a celeb. More than a few well-known brides (includes Queen Maxima of the Netherlands and Anne Hathaway) have tied the knot in a Valentino gown. Valentino himself even had a cameo alongside Meryl Streep in *The Devil Wears Prada*. He sold his empire in 2008 but they kept his name and he still often makes an appearance on the catwalk at big shows. *Via Condotti 12–13 | Metro A Spagna | Centro | ▥ E7*

FINE FOODS

ANTICA CACIARA TRASTEVERINA

How good is that **INSIDER TIP** cheese? On Saturdays, **Best of the buffalo** make sure you get to this 100 year old shop early, or else their amazing ricottas (made from sheep and goat milk) and real mozzarella di bufala will be sold out. You can console yourself with Sardinian pecorino, different varieties of salami or the San Daniele hams – even tastier than fine Parma ham according to real foodies. *Via San Francesco a Ripa 140 | FB: anticacaciara. it | tram 8 | bus H | Trastevere | ⌑ D10*

ANTICA SALUMERIA

Roman delicacies including sheep's and goat's cheese, Parma ham, olives, top wine and delicious pizza. *Piazza della Rotonda 3 / Pantheon | bus 40, 62, 64, 81 | Centro | ⌑ E8*

ENOTECA ANTICA

A distinguished shop dating from 1905 and selling vintage champagne, red and white wine and rare liqueurs. You can taste the wines and eat a snack. *Via della Croce 76b | Metro A Spagna | Centro | ⌑ E7*

EST ARTIGIANI DEL GUSTO

Figgy mustard, truffle sauce, matured ham, cheese, organic olive oil: the finest Italian products are on sale here, and they all make great presents. *Via dell'Orso 71 | bus 81, 492 | Centro | ⌑ D7*

FOCACCI

Focacci stocks treats like dried ceps, truffles, olive oil, wine and grappa. *Via della Croce 43 | Metro A Spagna | Centro | ⌑ E7*

VOLPETTI

Rome's top chefs come here to buy excellent ingredients: a full range of Italian cheeses and hams, and olive oil of the finest quality. The *Taverna Volpetti* offers (reasonably) good-value lunch

INSIDER TIP
Gourmet alert

Rummage for clothes, art and bric-a-brac at the Porta Portese flea market

The Fendi sisters' boutique combines luxury with cool design

around the corner. *Via Marmorata 47 | Metro B Piramide | bus 8, 23, 30, 75, 280 | tram 3 | Testaccio | ▢ E12*

GIFTS

ALDO FEFE ★

This shop for classy stationery and bookbinding has been in business since 1932. Aldo, the owner, produces personalised books, albums or frames within two days. *Via della Stelletta 20b | bus 62, 64, 81, 87 | Centro | ▢ E7*

BOTTEGA DEL MARMORARO

It's always worth visiting this workshop and its charming owner, sculptor Sandro Fiorentini. If he isn't working on his marble statues, Sandro will gladly carve your name or favourite saying on a marble tablet that you can collect the next day (from 15 euros) (including in Roman cuneiform script, Asterix style). The opening hours for the workshop are flexible but he is usually there Tue–Sat 9am–7.30pm. *Via Margutta 53b | Metro A Spagna | Centro | ▢ E6*

CAMPO MARZIO DESIGN

Expensive fountain pens, travel accessories, handbags and little notebooks made from top-quality leather. This local institution on the

INSIDER TIP
Posh pens in luxury leather

Campo Marzio (one of Rome's oldest districts) has been going strong since 1933. *Via di Campo Marzio 41 | campomarziodesign.it | bus 51, 62, 63, 80, 83, 85, 492* | Centro | ⊞ *E7*

OFFINCINA DELLA CARTA

Everything a calligrapher's heart could desire. Gaetana Gilardi's little shop is packed full of items from pretty letter-writing paper to diaries, notebooks, photo albums and calendars. As well as plenty of wrapping paper to transform them into perfect gifts. *Via Benedetta 26 B | bus H | tram 8 | Trastevere* | ⊞ *D9*

> **INSIDER TIP**
> **Hand-made and hand-bound**

PANDORA DELLA MALVA ★

Thousands of pretty things from cool present ideas to little charms, jewellery, lights, clutch bags and accessories. Pandora was the Greek goddess of gifts and giving. In real life she is called Donnatella and she has been producing her own stunning jewellery for 30 years using old coins and stone. Each piece is unique and the prices are fair too. *Piazza San Giovanni della Malva 3 | pandoradella malva.it | Bus H Tram 8 | Trastevere* | ⊞ *D9*

TECH IT EASY

An emporium for technogeeks: clocks that show different time zones, quirky bathroom scales, electronic knick-knacks. *Via del Gambero 1 and Via Arenula 34 | tech-it-easy.it | bus 52, 53, 61, 71, 80, 85, 117* | Centro | ⊞ *E8*

JEWELLERY

BIBELOT

If you like pretty accessories, Art Nouveau jewellery and Gallé vases, go and see the friendly sisters Valdete and Claudia. They also do jewellery repair. *Via Banchi Nuovi 2 | bus 40, 62, 64* | Centro | ⊞ *C8*

BULGARI

Perhaps you recognize the diamond-scaled reptile swallowing a one-carat dazzler … The Serpenti bracelet is one of many iconic pieces made by the luxury jeweller. Sometimes, however, Bulgari does something altogether different like the hugely expensive renovation and cleaning of the Spanish Steps and the Barcaccia Fountain on their doorstep. The window display is restrained as the real treasures are inside. *Via Condotti 10 | Metro A Spagna* | Centro | ⊞ *E7*

MELIS MASSIMO MARIA

Goldsmith Massimo uses 21-carat gold for pieces for his regular customers, and also produces modern items from 2,000-year-old coins. *Via dell'Orso 57 | bus 116* | Centro | ⊞ *C8*

R-01-IOS

The name may look like a code, but in fact it conceals the identity of Iosselliani's flagship store in Pigneto. Cool creations from the provocative pair Roberta and Paolo. Their other shop is in Tokyo. *Via del Pigneto 39a | iosselliani.com | tram 5, 19* | Centro | ⊞ *E7*

MARKETS & FLEA MARKETS

MERCATINO FLAMINIO

Clothes as far as the eye can see, including vintage fashion. This popular flea market consisting of around 240 stands is located north of the Piazza del Popolo. *Sun 10am–7pm, closed in Aug | admission 1.60 euros | Piazza della Marina 32 | tram 2, 19 | Flaminio | ⌖ D5*

PORTA PORTESE ★

You can find almost anything here – possibly even your stolen wallet … most likely empty. Hats, shoes, binoculars, watches and fun clothing. But watch out for pickpockets! *Sun 7am–2pm | between Viale Trastevere and Porta Portese | bus H, 780 | tram 3, 8 | Trastevere | ⌖ D11*

ORGANIC & ECO PRODUCTS

ALBERO DEL PANE

Rome's oldest organic shop has all kinds of sustainable foodstuffs, juices, vegetables and washing powders and detergents, as well as a big range of natural cosmetics. *Via Santa Maria del Pianto 19–20 | romabiologica.com | tram 8 | bus H, 30, 63, 780 | Centro | ⌖ E9*

ANTICA ERBORISTERIA ROMANA

Founded in 1752, Rome's oldest herbal pharmacy has always offered alternative medicines and the panelling inside is beautiful. *Via di Torre Argentina 15 | bus 40, 62, 64 | Centro | ⌖ E8–9*

DIMENSIONE NATURA

This fashion shop near the Fontana delle Tartarughe on Piazza Mattei aims to marry sustainable textiles made from cashmere, alpaca, linen and silk with chic Roman style. *Via dei Falegnami 66a | dimensionenatura. eu | tram 8 | bus 30, 40, 63, 64, 70 | Centro | ⌖ C8*

ORGANIC MARKET AT THE SLAUGHTERHOUSE

Il Mattatoio, the former slaughterhouse, could not get much greener. Every Sunday from 10am–5pm organic farmers sell their fresh vegetables, olive oil, honey and home-made pasta here. *Piazza Orazio Giustiniani 4 | bus 23, 780 | Testaccio | ⌖ D12–13*

ORGANIC MARKET DELLA MORETTA

Twice a month, organic farmers from the surrounding area sell their products: fruit, vegetables, honey, cheese, wine and olive oil. (The nearby Campo de' Fiori is also transformed into an organic market every third Sunday in the month.) *2nd and 4th Sun, 9am–5pm | Vicolo della Moretta | bus 62, 64 | tram 8 | Centro | ⌖ C8*

PEPERITA E IL CAVALLINO

After a spicy souvenir? Organic farmer Rita Salvadori grows hundreds of different types of chillies on her estate, while her sister Romina looks after the olive trees and produces the prize-winning olive oil "Il Cavallino". Both products are available from the shop in the Jewish quarter near Piazza Mattei. *Via della Reginella 30 |*

Bulgari offers its clients jewellery, watches, accessories and VIP status

ilcavallino.it | peperita.it | tram 8 |
Centro | ⌘ E9

SHOES

BARRILÀ

The name sounds like a brand of spaghetti, but this place is all about shoes. Their simple pumps and ballet flats will allow you to cope with even the most uneven Roman cobblestones. Their sandals in all colours of the rainbow are a hit and sell out quickly. The small boutique is slightly too crammed, but that shouldn't dissuade you! *Via del Babuino 33a* | *Metro A Spagna* | *Centro* | ⌘ E6

BORINI

Shoes, almost too good to wear: this is a shoemaker for Rome's poshest circles. *Via dei Pettinari 86* | *bus 23, 116* | *tram 8* | *Centro* | ⌘ D9

TOD'S

Diego della Valle is celebrated as the inventor of the elegant *gommini* loafers with distinctive stitching, with which he founded the famous brand Tod's. He made headlines as a patron of the arts by donating 25 million euros to the restoration of the crumbling Colosseum. *Via Fontanella Borghese 56/57 (Largo Goldoni)* | *bus 52, 53, 63* | *Centro* | ⌘ E7

NIGHTLIFE

Balmy evenings are spent in the open-air 'museum' of central Rome, between the Vatican, the Spanish Steps and the Pantheon: from April to October, Roman nightlife takes to the small streets of the Centro Storico.

Although there are numerous bars, cafés, wine bars and clubs, Romans prefer to stroll with friends *in corso* through the back streets of the historic centre – past stunningly lit-up ancient monuments and sparkling fountains that you can drink from before stopping for an ice cream at one of the many popular *gelaterie*.

The top places to wander are the centre and Trastevere. Monte Testaccio has also kept the charm of Ancient Rome and remains a trendy area. The same goes for the workers' and students' quarter of San Lorenzo, as well as Monti, Ostiense and Pigneto, which is situated on the arterial Prenestina and Casilina roads.

You can find out more about all events at comune.roma.it, oggi roma.it and abcroma.com or in *Trova Roma,* the Thursday supplement of *La Repubblica.*

WHERE ROME PARTIES

Villa Glori

📍 **Auditorium Parco della Musica ★**

Viale Maresciallo Pilsudski

TRIONFALE

Lungotevere Flaminio

PINCIANO

Fontana di Piazza Mazzini

Villa Borghese

Circonvallazione Trionfale

📍 **Alexanderplatz ★**

Via Cola di Rienzo

SALARIO

CITTÀ DEL VATICANO

Castel S. Angelo

Lungotevere Marzio

San Pietro

Lungotevere dei Tebaldi

Corso Vittorio Emanuele II

Via di Porta Cavalleggeri

TRASTEVERE

Classic nightlife scene, with wine bars, pubs and cafés

Cavour 313 ★ 📍

Monte Capitolino

Colosseo Ⓜ

AURELIO

📍 **Ombre Rosse ★**

Foro Romano

PALATINO

Villa Doria Pamphili

Via Guido Cavalcanti

Via dei Cerchi

Circo Massimo Ⓜ

Viale di Trastevere

Viale Aventino

TESTACCIO

Discos and bars keep things lively here

Via Marmorata

Lungotevere Testaccio

Caruso Caffè ★ 📍 **Caffè Latino ★**

Ⓜ Piramide

Via Olimpia

Circonvallazione Gianicolense

Via del Porto Fluviale

TIBURTINO

PIGNETO
Hip neighbourhood, with underground music venues, cafés and bars

Cars were once reepaired at Freni e Frizioni, but now it's a hangout for young Romans

BARS, CAFÉS & WINE BARS

Most clubs charge admission, or "membership fee" (*tessera*) which is usually around 15 euros, or sometimes as much as 20–30 euros. Very occasionally your first drink is free.

BAR DEL CINQUE

In Trastevere people love to drop in on this tiny corner bar. Good music and fun vibes especially when Alessandro, the barista, starts putting whisky into the hot chocolate. *Daily 6.30pm–2am | Vicolo del Cinque 5 | Bus 23, 280, H | tram 8 | Trastevere | D9*

INSIDER TIP
Hot chocolate with a kick

BAR DEL FICO

Relaxed and authentic bar on a beautiful small piazza, not too far from Piazza Navona. The ultimate meeting point for the trendy crowd. *Daily 8–2am | Piazza del Fico 26 | bus 64, 71, 81, 492 | Centro | D8*

BUM BUM DI MEL

Copacabana on the Tiber and Rome's coolest "minibar". A tiny spot in Trastevere is where Brazilian Mel mixes the best tropical cocktails including *caipirinhas*, *caipiroscas* and *mojitos*. Young Romans wait for ages in a queue to get one of her drinks and (illegally) sip it outside. *Daily 6pm–1am | Via del Moro 17 | Tram 8 | bus H, 780 | Trastevere | D10*

CAFFÈ LATINO ★

Buzzing location in the vaults of Monte Testaccio. Popular among Rome's *movida*. Often live reggae, house, jazz and blues sets. *Tue–Sun | Via di Monte Testaccio 96 | tel.*

0 65 78 24 11 | FB: caffelatinodroma | Metro B Piramide | bus 83, 121, 673 | Testaccio | ⌒ D–E12

CAVOUR 313 ★

A hip wine bar with stylish people, tasty snacks and fresh salads. *Daily, closed Sun in summer | Via Cavour 313 | tel. 0 66 78 54 96 | cavour313.it | Metro B Via Cavour | Monti | ⌒ G9*

CUL DE SAC

Narrow, wood-panelled rooms which really are reminiscent of a dead-end road. This used to be an old school Roman wine and olive store and it still offers a fantastic array of *vini* with up to 1,500 mainly Italian wines on offer. Popular rendezvous. *Daily | Piazza Pasquino 73 | bus 40, 62, 64 | tram 8 | Centro | ⌒ D8*

ENOTECA IL PICCOLO

Crowds of locals can be seen both in and outside this bar. It's a place where you can hang out while watching the world go by. Enjoy a *caffè* during the day or an evening drink. Excellent wine list, dry Prosecco, and strong Aperol Spritz. *Daily noon–midnight | Via del Governo Vecchio 74 | bus 40, 62, 64 | Centro | ⌒ D8*

FONCLEA

A favourite among Prati's live music bars. Jazz, rock, Dixie blues and funk every night. In summer it moves to the banks of the river under the Ponte Palatino *(Lungotevere degli Anguillara). (⌒ E10) Daily | Via Crescenzio 82 | fonclea.it | bus 34, 49, 87, 492 | ⌒ C7*

FRENI E FRIZIONI

Until recently this was a little car repair shop in Trastevere where *freni e frizioni* (brakes and clutches) were fixed. Now it's a popular bar. *Daily | Via del Politeama 4–6 | bus 23, 280, H | tram 8 | Trastevere | ⌒ D10*

JONATHAN'S ANGELS

Owner Jonathan has painted lavish frescoes on the walls of this popular bar near the Piazza Navona – even in the toilets! *Tue–Sun | Via della Fossa 16 | bus 62, 64 | Centro | ⌒ D8*

LEMONCOCCO

This is no trendy cocktail bar, it's just an old-fashioned, city kiosk on the Piazza Buenos Aires. Trams clatter past and the enchanting Art Nouveau buildings of Coppedè provide a glorious backdrop. But for many Romans, Lemoncocco means the taste of summer, sunshine and frivolity. They only serve one drink: sweet coconut milk with freshly squeezed Sicilian lemon juice. This recipe to success is apparently 70 years old. Gian Luca, the friendly *barista* won't reveal anything else.

> **INSIDER TIP** Suburban dolce vita

WHERE TO START?

Pigneto is the place to be. Around Via Pigneto (⌒ M10) there are more film clubs, book bars and cool clubs than anywhere else. The best way to get there is the newly completed C line on the Metro but there are plenty of taxis too.

A glass of *lemoncocco* costs 2.50 euros, with a shot (gin or vodka) 4.50 euros. *Mon–Fri 10.30–2am, Sat/Sun 4pm–2am | Piazza Buenos Aires | bus 83 | tram 3, 19 | Trieste | ⅏ H4*

OMBRE ROSSE ★

Aperitifs served with nibbles like *bruschetta*, *pizzette* or nuts. Pasta dishes like *spaghetti cacio e pepe* are simple, tasty and very reasonably priced.It's pleasant square to linger in and is at the heart of the nightlife quarter, Trastevere. Extremely friendly service. From September to April live music on Thursday evenings (jazz, blues, Mardi Gras). *Mon–Sat 11–2am | Piazza Sant'Egidio 12 | bus H, 23, 280 | tram 8 | Trastevere | ⅏ D10*

RIVE GAUCHE 2

A cross between a café, pub and club in studenty San Lorenzo. A homely feel with an excellent selection of craft beers. Happy hour till 9pm. *Daily | Via dei Sabelli 43 | tel. 0 64 45 67 22 | tram 3, 19 | bus 71, 30 | San Lorenzo | ⅏ L8*

CLUBS

ALEXANDERPLATZ ★

Italy's oldest jazz club where for more than 50 years almost all the greats have played is still swinging in Prati. Food and drinks leave a bit to be desired. *Mon–Sat | admission 15 euros | Via Ostia 9 | alexanderplatz jazzclub.com | Metro A Ottaviano–San Pietro | tram 19 | bus 492, 495 | Prati | ⅏ A–B6*

L'ALIBI

Rome's oldest gay disco with an enormous dance floor and roof terrace. You can have a film made of yourself dancing and download it at home. *Thu–Sat | Via di Monte Testaccio 44 | tel. 0 65 74 34 48 | Metro B Piramide | bus 23, 30 | Testaccio | ⅏ D13*

BLACKOUT

As the name implies: black is what the teenagers here wear, and the music is dark too mainly featuring punk, rock, grunge and house. *Tue–Sat | Via Casilina 713 | tel. 0 62 41 50 47 | bus 105 | Tuscolano | ⅏ M10*

CARUSO CAFFÈ ★

Fiesta, live bands, the hot tip for salsa, merengue, tango or Cuban son. Most Thursdays the band *Chirimia* plays. *Tue–Sun 11pm–4am | Via del Monte Testaccio 36 | carusocafe.com | bus 95, 170, 781 | Testaccio | ⅏ D13*

CASA DEL JAZZ

Once the home to a mafia boss, his confiscated villa and park is now a venue for jazz, jam sessions and festivals. *Viale di Porta Ardeatina 55 | tel. 06 70 47 31 | casajazz.it | Metro B Piramide | bus 30, 714 | Ardeatino | ⅏ F12*

INSIDER TIP
Where the Godfather lived

EX DOGANA

An old train depot in the industrial part of San Lorenzo has been turned into an underground venue for hipsters. It's a cool spot with a broad cultural programme including films, clubbing and gigs. Can be a bit chaotic. *Fri–Sun | Viale di Scalo di San Lorenzo 10 | exdogana.com | 14 Metro A San Giovanni | Tram 3, 19 | San Lorenzo | ☐ K9*

FANFULLA 101 ⭐

Pasolini, the eccentric 1960s film director would have loved this underground arts centre in Pigneto, his favourite quarter. Fanfulla prides itself on being inclusive and welcoming to all. Live indie, jazz, rock, pop and art-house films. *Daily | Via Fanfulla da Lodi 101 | fanfulla.org | bus 81, 105, 810 | Pigneto | ☐ M10*

GOA

This club in Ostiense is decked out in Bollywood style. It has a restaurant and cocktail bar too with lots of funk and house. *Tue–Sun | Via Libetta 13 | tel. 0 65 74 82 77 | goaclub.com | Metro B Garbatella | bus 23 | Ostiense | ☐ E15*

QUBE ⭐

A huge club in an old factory in Tiburtino, with a transgender night: RadioRock on Thursdays, a gay show *uccassassina* on Fridays and *Babylon for all* on Saturdays. *Wed–Sat | Via di Portonaccio 212 | tel. 06 43 85 44 50 | qubedisco.com | tram 5, 14, 19, get out at Prenestina/Via Portonaccio | bus 409 | Prenestino | ☐ 0*

RADIO LONDRA

This themed bar named after a Resistance radio station from the World War II is the definition of "in". The setting is an improvised air-raid shelter with sandbags lying all around. The bar staff wear helmets. *Wed–Sun | admission 15 euros | Via di Monte Testaccio 67 | radiolondradiscobar.com*

Nightlife in Testaccio: Disco Alibi

| *Metro B Piramide* | *bus 23, 30* | *Testaccio* | 🚇 *E13*

ROOM 26

An ambitious project created by a group of young art and music enthusiasts on the Piazza Marconi. It's all under one roof: from clubbing and a restaurant to modern art and photo exhibitions. *Thu–Sun* | *Piazza Marconi 31* | *EUR District* | *room26.it* | *bus 170, 791* | *EUR* | 🚇 *0*

CINEMAS

AZZURRO SCIPIONI

Well-loved art-house cinema with weeks devoted to avant-garde movies and international retrospectives, from Robert Altman to Akira Kurosawa and Luchino Visconti. Some screenings with subtitles. *Via degli Scipioni 82* | *silvanoagosti.com/cinemaazzurro* | *Metro A Lepanto* | *Prati* | 🚇 *C6*

INTRASTEVERE

Arty film club in an alley near Piazza Trilussa in Trastevere, which often screens films in English. *Vicolo Moroni 3a* | *intrastevere.cdr.18tickets.it* | *bus H, 23* | *tram 8* | *Trastevere* | 🚇 *D10*

NUOVO SACHER

The cult director Nanni Moretti's production company is called Sacher, and his own cinema, Nuovo Sacher, is a declaration of his love for the cake of that name. Outdoor cinema in summer. Sometimes events with directors. *Largo Ascianghi 1* | *tel. 0 65 81 81 16* | *sacherfilm.eu* | *tram 3, 8* | *bus 75, 780* | *Trastevere* | 🚇 *D11*

CONCERTS & MUSICALS THEATRE & OPERA

At last Rome can hold its head up to other great cities for classical music, theatre and opera thanks to the *Auditorium Parco della Musica*. And there are still plenty of orchestra and choir concerts held in fitting church settings especially in winter. Baroque churches such as 🔸 *Sant'Ignazio, Santa Maria del Popolo* and *Santa Maria in Aracoeli* offer free organ concerts and oratorios with a wonderful atmosphere. Sometimes the walls of the Pantheon reverberate to the sound of Gregorian chant. For opera and concert listings, see *musicaroma.it*

AUDITORIUM PARCO DELLA MUSICA ⭐

A spectacular new concert venue

Auditorium Parco della Musica: ultra-modern acoustic architecture by Renzo Piano

which seems to have got the whole world excited! During construction of the building, which was designed by Renzo Piano (of The Shard fame), the foundations of an ancient villa were discovered. They have been skilfully incorporated into the architecture.

The auditorium has three halls seating 2,800, 1,200 and 700 as well as an outdoor amphitheatre. There is also a cafeteria, a music museum and a large shop selling music and books, as well as a park with playground. *Park daily 11am–8pm | Viale Pietro de Coubertin 15 (near Stadio Flaminio) | tickets tel. 06 89 29 82, from abroad tel. +39 02 60 06 09 00 | box office daily 11am–8pm | listicket.it, auditorium.com | tram 2, 19 | bus 53, 910 | Flaminio | ⊞ D2*

TEATRO MARCELLO

Chamber concerts are held after dark in an enchantingly lit ancient amphitheatre. *Via del Teatro di Marcello 44 | tickets: classictic.com | bus 30, 63, 170 | Centro | ⊞ E9*

TEATRO DELL'OPERA

Previously seen as a bit mediocre, in 1990 the opera house in the *Terme di Caracalla (Centro | ⊞ G12)* was made world-famous by the three tenors, José Carreras, Plácido Domingo and Luciano Pavarotti.

Following a long closure the impressive Baths of Caracalla have reopened with lots of performances in summer. *Box office Mon–Sat 10am–6pm, Sun 9am–1.30pm | Piazza Beniamino Gigli 1 | operaroma.it, listicket.it | Metro A Repubblica | Monti | ⊞ G8*

ACTIVE &
RELAXED

Villa Lante

SPORT, ACTIVITIES & WELLNESS

FOOTBALL

What are the three things that get Italian men most passionate? Football, football and football. However, Roman *calcio* has recently gone through a series of scandals. Money has dried up, and clubs have had to boot many of their hooligan fans out of their stadiums.

However, the Stadio Olimpico is considered safe. It is shared by two Serie A teams: AS Roma and Lazio Roma. Real *tifosi* (fans) have their support for a club hardwired into their DNA. A supporter of Lazio who dons a sky-blue scarf to go to the match on Sunday would be unlikely to marry woman from a red-and-yellow-clad clan that supports AS Roma and vice versa.

If you want to experience true Roman *calcio*, give the *curva nord*, the north end that's occupied by militant Lazio fans and the *romanisti's* south stand wide berths. For fixtures and information, see *sslazio.it or asroma.it | no guided tours through the stadium.*

JOGGING & JOGGING TOURS

There is a lovely jogging route in the park of Villa Borghese. Set off from the Galleria Borghese and head towards the Pincio hill and then on to the church of Trinità dei Monti and back via Via Vittorio Veneto – or past the Galleria Nazionale d'Arte Moderna to the Etruscan museum in Villa Giulia, a distance of around three classically beautiful miles.

You can also explore the Centro Storico at a brisk pace by booking a personal trainer for a spot of *Sight Jogging (84 euros/hr | tel. 0 34 73 35 31 85 | sight jogging.it)*. The fit, multilingual guides will jog with you along ten cultural routes through the city,

INSIDER TIP
The early bird...

Ostia beach

even for early-bird tours at 6 or 7 in the morning, when the traffic is still tolerable and the real early birds are in full song.

OLYMPIAN SWIMMING

Romans have been swimming and bathing for thousands of years. And if you want something sportier than a spa, there is a 50m pool in the city. The *Piscina delle Rose (🕮 0) (day pass 16 euros | Metro B EUR Palasport)* is the pool used in the 1960 Olympics and is situated on the EUR site to the south of the city. Alongside swimming there is a gym and spa on offer (both of which have seen happier days). If you prefer a day at the seaside, then make your way to the Lido di Ostia (see p.146). The train out there costs just 1.50 euros but the beach clubs are extremely expensive. Two loungers and a parasol will set you back at least 30 euros.

SPAS

If you would like to treat yourself after the rigours of sightseeing, the *Centro Benessere (🕮 E6) (Via del Babuino 9 | tel. 06 32 88 88 20 | Metro A Flaminio | bus 117, 119, 490)* in the De Russie luxury hotel is a place to be pampered while hobnobbing with Rome's high society: sauna, gym and saltwater jacuzzi for approx. 45 euros; shiatsu massage and facials for around 75 euros. Book in advance.

More indulgence for body and soul is on offer at the *Acanto Day Spa (🕮 E8) (Piazza Rondanini 30 | tel. 06 68 30 06 64 | acantospa.it | bus 70, 81, 87, 116, 492)*, where guests enjoy Asian tea, Thai massages and ethereal scents. From 70 euros.

FESTIVALS & EVENTS

JANUARY

The good witch **Befana** brings well-behaved Roman children presents on 6 January. In her honour, the Piazza Navona is transformed into a fairground.

FEBRUARY

Carnevale: Rome celebrates on a grand scale. Colombina, Arlecchino and other *commedia dell'arte* characters take over Piazza Navona while children celebrate in Villa Borghese Park.

MARCH/APRIL

Rome Marathon *(maratonadiroma. it)*: runs through the Centro Storico on the penultimate Sunday in March.

Urbi et Orbi: on Easter Sunday, the Pope's address and blessing, brings hundreds of thousands of pilgrims to St Peter's Square. Romans tend to head to the countryside on Easter Monday (*pasquetta*).

APRIL

Festa d'Arte: art fair on Via Margutta.

Rome's Birthday: the idea Rome was founded in 753 BCE is an myth but it does not stop the whole city celebrating on 21 April with concerts, fireworks and street parties.

Festa delle Azalee: a celebration of the azaleas that adorn the Spanish Steps from mid-April to mid-May, and lots of fashion shows.

MAY

Festa del Popolo: on 1 May (International Labour Day), there is a large demonstration on the Piazza del Popolo in the morning and a pop concert afterwards.

Mostra dell'Antiquariato: antiques fair on Via dei Coronari (also in September).

Concorso Ippico Internazionale: horse racing on the Piazza di Sienna in Villa Borghese Park.

Festa della Repubblica

JUNE

Festa della Repubblica: a military parade on Via dei Fori Imperiali (2 June).

Feast of St Anthony of Padua: mass on Via Merulana (13 June).

San Giovanni Fair: St John's Day in the Lateran calendar (24 June)

29 June: **Festival of the City's Patrons, St Peter and St Paul** is celebrated with a papal mass in St Peter's when the faithful kiss the feet of St Peter's statue.

JUNE–SEPTEMBER

Estate Romana *(www.estateromana. it)*: jazz, concerts, outdoor cinema and fashion shows.

JULY

Festa de Noantri: public festival in Trastevere with a procession of the Madonna.

Tevere Expo: fair of the Italian regions on the bank of the Tiber with music, ballet and folklore.

AUGUST

Ferragosto: the Day of Assumption (15 August) is mostly celebrated by tourists as Romans tend to go on holiday.

SEPTEMBER

Notte Bianca: museum night with concerts, dance, theatre on the second or third Saturday.

RomaEuropa: festival of music, theatre and dance from EU member states.

NOVEMBER

RomFilmFestival: film showcase in the Parco della Musica auditorium.

DECEMBER

Feast of the Immaculate Conception: papal prayers on the Piazza di Spagna (8 December).

SLEEP WELL

SLEEK DESIGN AT HOTEL ART

The Via Margutta, an arty street at the foot of the Pincio, was once Rome's Montmartre. It is where artists and artisans had their workshops and boutiques and where painters like Renato Guttuso and Giorgio de Chirico practised their craft. It is fitting then that there is a *Hotel Art (47 rooms | Via Margutta 56 | tel. 06 32 87 11 | hotelart.it | Metro A Spagna | €€€ | Northern Centro Storico | ⫞ E6)* here. Its cool design, fun bar and gym stay true to the artistic heritage of the area.

BREAKFAST BENEATH ORANGES

Peace and calm in the eye of the storm; even in buzzing Trastevere, there are quiet spots. One of these, which will appeal to anyone wanting to explore the area's nightlife as well as those who are more interested in seeing the sites, is the three-star *Santa Maria* hotel *(18 rooms. | Vicolo del Piede 2 | tel. 0 65 89 46 26 | htl santamaria.com | tram 8 | bus H | €€ | Trastevere | ⫞ D10)*. Housed in a 16th-century monastery, breakfast is served in a grand courtyard under the shade of orange trees.

IN THE EMPERORS' BACKYARD

A hotel haunted by Roman emperors? The weak and curmudgeonly Emperor Nerva did one good thing in his life – he adopted the General Trajan and nominated him his successor. *Hotel Nerva (19 Zi. | Via Tor dei Conti 3 | tel. 0 66 78 18 35 | hotelnerva.com | Metro B Cavour | bus 75 | €€ | Southern Centro Storico | ⫞ F9)* takes its name from the hapless emperor and is located near Trajan's Forum and his column. The Roman Forum and the Colosseum are also just a stone's throw away. If you have had enough of history, the buzzing area of Monti is just round the corner.

Lobby at the Hotel Art

ROME'S MOST FAMOUS CRIME SCENE

It's true, the entrance door is small and the lobby is unspectacular. But the rooms in the *Teatro di Pompeo (28 rooms | Largo Pallaro 8 | tel. 06 68 30 01 70 | www.hotelteatrodi-pompeo.it | bus 40, 60, 64)* are comfortable and homely – and you will sleep soundly above the walls of the ancient theatre, where Julius Caesar is said to have been murdered (among five other possible locations) 2,000 years ago. Campo de' Fiori, Piazza Navona, the Ghetto and other major sights are close by.

A MONASTIC RETREAT

Solo donne is the motto in the *Orsa Maggiore* women's hostel (singles from 60 euros, doubles from 75 euros, beds in 5-bed dorms from 26 euros/night, cheaper in the off season | Via San Francesco di Sales 1a/Via della Lungara | tel. 0 66 89 37 53 | orsamaggioreroma.com | bus 23, 280 | €€ | Trastevere | ⌕ C9), which is located in an old monastery in Trastevere. The rooms are named after female characters from Greek mythology, from Andromeda to Aprhrodite.

A NOBLE LEGACY

In the 17th century, the childless Donna Camilla Savelli founded an orphanage for noble daughters in a spot above Trastevere and commissioned Francesco Borromini, the master of baroque, to design it. Today it is a hotel, *Donna Camilla Savelli (55 rooms | Via Garibaldi 27 | tel. 06 58 88 61 | hoteldonnacamilla savelli.com | bus 23, 280 | €€€ | Trastevere | ⌕ C10)* with beautiful stuccowork, a roof garden and a quiet courtyard.

INSIDER TIP Perfect hillside palazzo

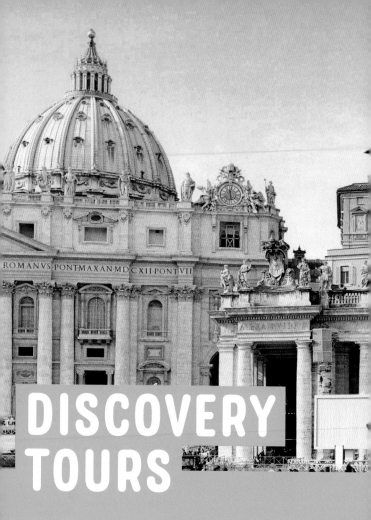

DISCOVERY TOURS

Want to get under the skin of the city? Then our discovery tours provide the perfect guide – they include advice on which sights to visit, tips on where to stop for that perfect holiday snap, a choice of the best places to eat and drink and suggestions for fun activities.

Piazza San Pietro

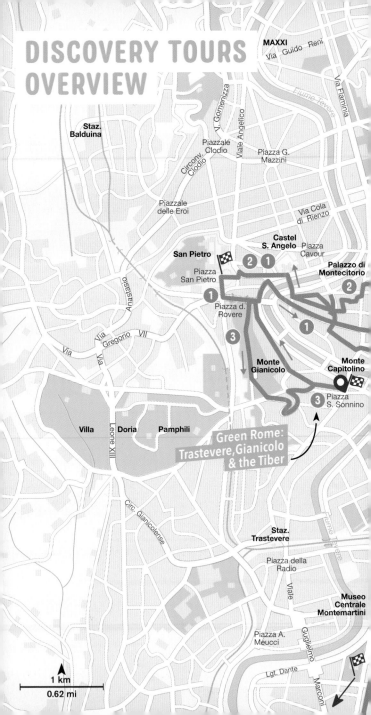

DISCOVERY TOURS OVERVIEW

MAXXI

Via Guido Reni

Fiume Tevere

Via Flaminia

Staz.
Balduina

V. Gomenizza

Piazzale
Clodio

Viale Angelico

Piazza G.
Mazzini

Circonv. Clodio

Piazzale
delle Eroi

Via Cola
di Rienzo

Castel
S. Angelo

Piazza
Cavour

San Pietro 🏁

Piazza
San Pietro

Palazzo di
Montecitorio

Via Anastasio

Via Gregorio VII

Via

Piazza d.
Rovere

Monte
Gianicolo

Monte
Capitolino

Piazza
S. Sonnino

Villa   Doria   Pamphili

Leone XIII

Green Rome:
Trastevere, Gianicolo
& the Tiber

Circ. Gianicolense

Staz.
Trastevere

Fiume Tevere

Piazza della
Radio

Viale

Museo
Centrale
Montemartini

Guglielmo

Piazza A.
Meucci

Lgt. Dante

Marconi

🏁

1 km
0.62 mi

① ROME IN A DAY

➤ Where the emperor's thumb decided on life or death
➤ Where Caesar and Cicero went to work
➤ Where Rome stretches out beneath you

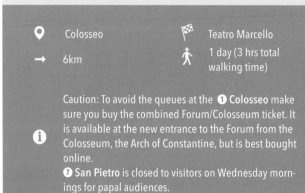

📍 Colosseo

→ 6km

🏁 Teatro Marcello

🚶 1 day (3 hrs total walking time)

ℹ️ Caution: To avoid the queues at the ① **Colosseo** make sure you buy the combined Forum/Colosseum ticket. It is available at the new entrance to the Forum from the Colosseum, the Arch of Constantine, but is best bought online.
⑦ San Pietro is closed to visitors on Wednesday mornings for papal audiences.

WHERE GLADIATORS BATTLED

① Colosseum

Slept well? Camera at the ready? Then start the day at the ① Colosseum ➤ p. 30. If you've already bought the combined Forum/Colosseum ticket online, then you'll barely have to queue to see this spectacular ancient monument. *At the entrance near the Arch of Constantine*, legionnaires normally stand around in costume, ready to pose for a photo. Careful though – they charge exorbitant prices! Your next stop is ancient too because the ② Roman Forum ➤ p. 32 is close by. *The Via Sacra takes you to the centre of power in Ancient Rome. At the Arco di Settimo Severo head left and climb up to the new exit of the Forum below the Capitol.* You have now reached the ③ Capitoline Hill ➤ p. 37, the heart of Rome, with its Piazza del Campidoglio designed by Michelangelo. The statue of Emperor Marcus Aurelius on the oval plazza is just a copy, the original stands majestically in the Musei Capitolini ➤ p. 37 – you should save a visit there for another day.

② Roman Forum

③ Capitoline Hill

Are you ready for a coffee? Then, stop for a cappuccino in the ❹ Caffè Capitolino *(Tue–Sun 9.30am–7pm | Piazzale Caffarelli 4)* above the museum, which also has a fabulous rooftop terrace. You don't need a museum ticket to get to it, simply *walk to the right round the palazzo to the side entrance, and then climb the steps to the terrace.* If you want to climb higher for an even more sensational view of the Eternal City, then *from Piazza Venezia take the entrance* into the snow-white ❺ Monumento Nazionale a Vittorio Emanuele II ➤ p. 39. On the right-hand side and slightly hidden, you will find a glass lift *(7 euros)* that transports you high up to the Quadriga where the domes, churches and palazzi of Rome lie at your feet.

Has Ancient Rome woken your appetite? Then treat yourself in the ❻ Terre e Domus Enoteca *(Mon–Sat 7.30am–midnight | Foro Traiano 82/Via dei Fori Imperiali | €–€€)* to hearty regional cuisine from Latium Province. This is the only good restaurant near the forums, so it gets very full at lunch. The wine is excellent here, but you still have a lot to see. St Peter's is waiting! *From Piazza Venezia (bus stop Via del Plebiscito), take bus 64*

❹ Caffè Capitolino

❺ Monumento Nazionale a Vittorio Emanuele II

❻ Terre e Domus Enoteca

Bernini's angels lead the way to Castel Sant'Angelo

in the direction of the Stazione San Pietro and hop off at Cavalleggeri/San Pietro.

VISIT FRANCIS, THE PAPAL POPSTAR, AT ST PETER'S

And here it is, one of Christendom's most imposing churches: 7 San Pietro ➤ p. 60. Every Wednesday, throngs of Catholics assemble in front of it, on the Bernini-designed Piazza San Pietro – with its elegant colonnades – for an audience with the Pope. *You'll see the security checks for St Peter's Basilica in the colonnade on your right.* To visit the Vatican Museums ➤ p. 62 and the Sistine Chapel ➤ p. 58 you would arrive from the right of the Vatican ensemble, but you should plan an extra day for this – the treasures will otherwise play havoc with your timetable. To reach **8** Castel Sant'Angelo ➤ p. 66 and its splendid view over the city, *walk along the Via della Conciliazione.* Once you've been inspired by Bernini's elegant angel statues – and pestered by the street sellers – *take the Ponte Sant'Angelo back into the Centro Storico. From the Via del Spirito Santo, head along the* **9** Via dei Banchi Nuovi, a pretty street with small jewellery shops such as Bibelot ➤ p. 105, as well as gold-leaf frame makers, antique shops, cafés and trattorias. *Follow the equally lively Via del Governo Vecchio to* Il Pasquino, one of the famous talking statues, the 👥 *statue parlanti.* From there, it is just a few metres to the magnificent **10** Piazza Navona ➤ p. 45. If you are wilting by this stage, a *gelato,* from a place like Grom ➤ p. 84, or a *caffè* enjoyed in the midst of a buzzing crowd will liven you up again.

8 Castel Sant'Angelo

9 Via dei Banchi Nuovi

10 Piazza Navona

THE HEART OF ROME'S JEWISH COMMUNITY

To finish your day, *stroll along the Via della Cuccagna and the Via dei Baullari to* **11** Campo de' Fiori ➤ p. 44, where you can order an *aperitivo* and linger in wonderful surroundings until dinner as this is the rendezvous for the Roman *ragazzi.* By 8pm the many trattorias of the district will be filling up. If you are also hungry, *go along the Via dei Giubbonari* and, when you pass the Via Arenula, you'll enter the picturesque Ghetto with its revived Roman-Jewish scene. *From the Via dei Falegnami, take a detour to the* Fontana delle Tartarughe ➤ p. 51 on the Piazza Mattei. *Back on the Via Portico d'Ottavia* try some Roman and Jewish specialities at **12** Ristorante Il Giardino Romano *(closed Wed | Via del Portico d'Ottavia 18 | tel. 06 68 80 96 61 | €€).* After a good meal, *stroll through the Portico d'Ottavia,* which Emperor Augustus had built for his sister Ottavia in 27 CE, to the illuminated **13** Teatro Marcello ➤ p. 51, where classical concerts are held in summer.

11 Campo de' Fiori

12 Ristorante Il Giardino Romano

13 Teatro Marcello

❷ BAROQUE TOUR: FROM THE VILLA BORGHESE TO ST PETER'S SQUARE

➤ Barefoot in the park: Villa Borghese and Bernini's models
➤ Competitive creators: Bernini vs Borromini
➤ Rome's best espresso (apparently)

📍 Galleria Borghese   🏁 St Peter's

→ 6.7km   🚶 4 hrs (2 hrs total walking time)

ℹ️ Reservation necessary for ❶ Galleria Borghese (*ticketeria.it*)
Caution: ⓰ Piazza San Pietro and ⓱ San Pietro are closed on Wednesday mornings for papal audiences.

❶ Galleria Borghese

❷ Villa Borghese

❸ Piazza Barberini

BERNINI'S STUNNING NUDES IN THE GALLERIA BORGHESE

Start your tour at the wonderful ❶ Galleria Borghese ➤ p. 57 *(online booking only)*, the best place for getting an impression of Bernini's early works as a sculptor from the somewhat clumsy looking *David* to the radiant nakedness of *Apollo and Daphne. Stroll through the gardens of the* ❷ Villa Borghese ➤ p. 57 *and enjoy a cappuccino in the* Cinecaffè *(daily 9am–9pm | Largo Marcello Mastroianni 1 | €–€€). Next, head along the Via Veneto,* the street for exclusive cafés, hotels and the *dolce vita,* to ❸ Piazza Barberini, where Bernini immortalised his name more than once: at the corner of Via Veneto and Via Basilio is the Fontana delle Api (bee fountain); three bees were the heraldic symbol of the Barberini pope family. On the piazza, Bernini's elegant Fontana del Tritone with its sensuous Neptune seems to spread a feeling of lightness of being.

When you turn into the steep *Via Quattro Fontane,* you'll notice on your left the three-storey façade of the ④ Palazzo Barberini. Begun by Borromini, it was finished by Bernini, who triumphantly brought together several kinds of columns. Today the palace is the Galleria Nazionale d'Arte Antica a Palazzo Barberini *(Tue–Sun 8.30am–7pm | admission 7 euros). At the crossing with four fountains, turn into the long Via Quirinale,* where there is another example of the toxic but creative rivalry between the two architects. In the little church ⑤ San Carlo ➤ p. 58, often nicknamed San Carlino by the Romans, Borromini, with sparing use of materials, designed a graceful but austerely composed oval interior that creates an illusion of height. As usual, his rival Bernini went all out by contrast. *Less than 200m away,* the two-storey ⑥ Sant'Andrea al Quirinale ➤ p. 58, a popular church for weddings, is also oval (but rotated through 90 degrees) and has an impressive, monumental entrance and steps. Beyond it is the massive and ancient Fontana dei Dioscuri, on which the colossal statues of Castor and

INSIDER TIP
Egyptian souvenir

④ Palazzo Barberini

⑤ San Carlo

⑥ Sant'Andrea al Quirinale

Pollux, taken from the Baths of Constantine, hold on to an obelisk that Emperor Augustus brought back from Egypt as a souvenir.

⑦ Piazza del Quirinale

From the ⑦ Piazza del Quirinale you can enjoy great views of the city before *passing the Palazzo del Quirinale and descending the flat steps of the Via Dataria* until you hear the splashing of the ⑧ Fontana di Trevi ➤ p. 52. Rome's most sensuous fountain was built by Nicolas Salvi, but did you know that the designs were drawn up by a certain Bernini? *Head across the Piazza Colonna with its column of Marcus Aurelius – and you are now in the political heart of modern Italy.* Pass the *Palazzo Chigi*, the seat of government, and continue to ⑨ Palazzo Montecitorio, adorned with obelisks and a curving façade designed by Bernini in 1655. The palazzo appears on TV every evening on the Italian news as it now houses the parliament. *Time for ice cream? Take a slight detour over the Piazza Montecitorio to the Via Uffici del Vicario* and head directly to the ⑩ Gelateria Giolitti ➤ p. 83, Rome's oldest ice-cream shop.

⑧ Fontana di Trevi

⑨ Palazzo Montecitorio

⑩ Gelateria Giolitti

PIAZZO NAVONA: BAROQUE'S BEST ARENA

Onwards to the Pantheon ➤ p. 48 and the small and intimate ⑪ Piazza Sant'Eustachio, with its namesake bar, which is said to have the best coffee in Rome. *Continue to the Corso Rinascimento*, from where you can enjoy a view of Borromini's bizarre masterpiece Sant'Ivo alla Sapienza. The church with its curved baroque façade has a bee-shaped floorplan. The architect hoped to flatter his pompous patron, Urban VIII with this reference to the heraldry of the Barberini family. *After crossing Corso Rinascimento you reach* ⑫ Piazza Navona ➤ p. 45, the centrepiece of which is Bernini's Fontana dei Quattro Fiumi. The church of Sant'Agnese is – you guessed it – by his enemy Borromini. *Leave the piazza along the Via Tor Milina and walk past an older artistic gem,* the church of Santa Maria della Pace ➤ p. 46 with Raphael's frescoes of the Sibyls. In the ⑬ Caffetteria Chiostro del Bramante ➤ p. 82, next door, you can browse through art books

⑪ Piazza Sant'Eustachio

⑫ Piazza Navona

⑬ Caffetteria Chiostro del Bramante

Gelateria Giolitti has served ice cream to the likes of Justin Timberlake and the Obamas

in the bookshop, visit an exhibition or simply enjoy some refreshment.

THE PONTE S'ANGELO: HEAVENLY BEINGS SHOW A LEG

Next take the Via dei Coronari, the street of antique dealers, *on your way to the Tiber.* Time for lunch? How about a *pranzo* at the ⑭ Osteria dell'Antiquariato *(daily | Piazzetta di San Simeone 26 | tel. 0 66 87 96 94 | €€)* on the pretty *Piazzetta di San Simeone?* Your route then takes you *over the Ponte Sant' Angelo,* completed in 136 CE by Emperor Hadrian to provide access to his mausoleum, on top of which stands the papal fortification ⑮ Castel Sant'Angelo ➤ p. 66. It was Bernini who turned the Ponte Sant' Angelo into Rome's most graceful bridge by adding serene statues of angels to whom he lent sensuous folds of drapery and an all too earthly flirtatious smile. The last stop on your walk is Bernini's most daring work (with the best of Christian intentions): the elliptical ⑯ Piazza San Pietro, which seems to embrace all of Christendom with open arms. You end

⑭ **Osteria dell'Antiquariato**

⑮ **Castel Sant'Angelo**

⑯ **Piazza San Pietro**

⑰ San Pietro

your tour in ⑰ San Pietro ➤ p. 60 standing under Bernini's bronze baldachin, a structure for which both architects should be given credit. Its famous volutes were in fact designed by Borromini (and helped make him famous) yet in those days the term copyright had not yet been invented: Bernini paid Borromini just a tenth of his fee for his work and threw him out shortly before the baldachin was completed..

❸ GREEN ROME: TRASTEVERE, GIANICOLO & THE TIBER

➤ Piazza with a café, cornettos and a cool church
➤ Acqua Paola: popes have always loved fountains
➤ A woman on horseback and a stupendous view of Rome

📍 Piazza Sonnino	🏁 Piazza Sonnino
↻ 5km	🚶 4 hrs (1½ hrs total walking time)

BRAMANTE'S TEMPIETTO – A POPULAR PLACE TO GET MARRIED

❶ Piazza Sonnino

❷ Piazza Santa Maria in Trastevere

❸ Caffè di Marzio

❹ Tempietto

Start your walk at the ❶ Piazza Sonnino in Trastevere, an old artisan's quarter. *Stroll along the Via della Lungaretta* until you reach ❷ Piazza Santa Maria in Trastevere, named after the oldest church in Rome that is dedicated to the Virgin Mary ➤ p. 70. The golden mosaic above the atrium sparkles as you approach. Time for breakfast? On the same square and popular with Romans, the ❸ Caffè di Marzio *(Thu-Mon 8am-2pm, Tue 10am-10pm | €-€€)* offers small snacks, fresh juices and cappuccino. *Follow the Via della Paglia and then Via Garibaldi* to the church ❹ Tempietto in the courtyard of the adjoining Franciscan monastery is a miniature masterpiece of High Renaissance architecture – and a great spot for (wedding) photos.

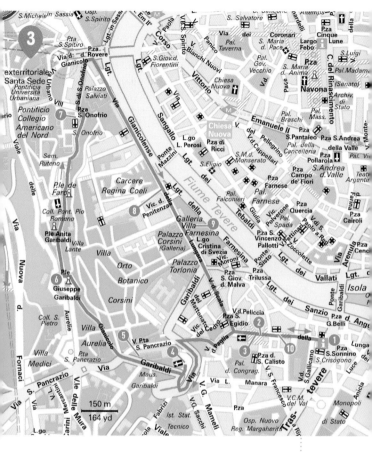

Continue on the Via Garibaldi taking the shortcut via the steps of San Pancrazio until you hear the rushing water of the ❺ *Fontana dell'Acqua Paola*. In 1612, Pope Paul V commissioned Carlo Maderno to build this monumental fountain which was supplied with water from a restored aqueduct from Ancient Roman times. *Head uphill on the very green Passeggiata del Gianicolo.* It is best to reach the ❻ *Piazza Garibaldi* before noon, when a very punctual cannon salute is fired just like in the olden days. The view from the square is stunning and Giuseppe Garibaldi (1807–82) Italy's most famous independence fighter, sits in its middle. *Follow the path*

❺ Fontana dell'Acqua Paola

❻ Piazza Garibaldi

One of Raphael's frescoes in the Galleria Villa Farnesina

through the gardens to a woman seated on a horse, a pistol in her hand and holding her son in her arms. There are bronze cavaliers over the world, but it's not often you see a statue of a female rider. This is Anita Garibaldi Ribeiro, Garibaldi's Brazilian wife, comrade-in-arms and mother of his children, with whom he travelled from country to country. There is another splendid view from the ❼ Sant'Onofrio church which also has a collection of baroque frescoes in its courtyard. *Now descend the Salita S. Onofrio to Piazza della Rovere, where the traffic and the Tiber await.*

❼ Sant'Onofrio church

BEAUTIFUL BAR IN A MONASTIC COURTYARD
Follow the Tiber until you reach the Palazzo Salviati where you turn right into the Via della Lungara. In an old monastic courtyard, you'll find the ❽ Luna e l'Altra *(Mon 8am–4pm, Tue–Sat 8.30am–10.30pm, Sun 8am–4pm | Via San Francesco di Sales 1a | €).* They serve organic coffee in the morning, vegetarian lunch (7–15 euros), aperitifs and an all-you-can-eat buffet (10 euros with a juice) in the evening. The bar belongs to the *Casa Internazionale delle Donne. Afterwards follow the Via*

❽ Luna e l'Altra

della Lungara until you reach the ❾ Galleria Nazionale Villa Farnesina ➤ p. 67. In the small yet exquisite Renaissance palace, take time to marvel at Raphael's frescoes *Cupid and Psyche*. The palace owner's mistress is said to have been one of the models. To complete your tour, *stroll along the Via della Scala to old Trastevere*. If you've only had time for a drink until now, enjoy a fresh salad, *bruschetta* or a plate of pasta in the lively ❿ Enoteca Trastevere *(daily noon–1am | Via della Lungaretta 86 | €)* before you return to the ❶ Piazza Sonnino.

> ❾ Galleria Nazionale Villa Farnesina

> ❶ Piazza Sonnino

❹ ANCIENT ROME BY BIKE: VIA APPIA ANTICA

➤ Travel back to Ancient Rome
➤ Above and below ground: graves, aqueducts and catacombs
➤ Where chariots once raced

📍	Via Appia Antica Information Office	🏁	Aquedotto dei Quintili
→	9km	🚲	4 hrs (total cycling time 1½ hrs)

ℹ A Sunday ride. Getting there: bus 218 (from San Giovanni in Laterano) or bus 118 (from Metro B: Circo Massimo) to the ❺ San Sebastiano catacombs; or taxi from San Giovanni in the Lateran to ❷ Quo Vadis catacombs; or taxi from San Giovanni in the Lateran to Kirche.

DISCOVER THE ROMAN PERIOD ON A BIKE
★ You can hire bicycles *(daily 9.30am–4.30pm | tel. 0 65 13 53 16 | www.parcoappiaantica.it)* at the ❶ Via Appia Antica Information Office *(Via Appia Antica 58–60)* opposite the little church ❷ Quo Vadis. According to the legend, St Peter, fleeing from Nero's

> ❶ Via Appia Antica Information Office
> ❷ Quo Vadis

executioners, encountered Christ here. When he asked "Lord, where are you going?" ("*Quo vadis?*"), he received the answer "To Rome, to be crucified a second time."

Once you have your bicycle and have adjusted your saddle, *don't take the Via Appia Antica but head on to the private road to its right* which goes over the green hill and leads you down to the catacombs. *Turning off into the Via Ardeatina takes you first to the* ❸ ✝ Calixtus Catacombs *(Thu-Tue 9am-noon and 2-5pm | admission 8 euros | Via Appia Antica 110-126)* and the ❹ ✝ Domitilla Catacombs *(Wed-Mon 9am-noon and*

❸ Kalixtus Catacombs

❹ Domitilla Catacombs

2.30–5pm | Via delle Sette Chiese 282 | Via Ardeatina).
Now head back to the Via Appia Antica and on to ❺ San
Sebastiano Fuori le Mura and to the Catacombs of
the Basilica di San Sebastiano (Mon–Sat 9am–12
noon, 2.30–5pm | 8 euros | Via Appia Antica 136).

❺ San Sebastiano
fuori le mura

On your left you will see one of the most splendid
archaeological monuments in the area: the ❻ Circo di
Massenzio, an ancient arena, and the ❼ Grave of
Romulus *(Tue–Sun 10am–4pm)*, not Romulus the
founder of the city, but a son of Emperor Maxentius
who died young in 309 CE. The most impressive building on the Via Appia is without a doubt the crenellated
❽ Mausoleo di Cecilia Metella, the grave of a rich
Roman woman and daughter of a general. Opposite
her mausoleum, you'll see a small fountain where you
can fill up your water bottles. The cobblestones on this
section of your tour date back 2,300 years! Top tip: Ride
along the green verges wherever possible. And don't
miss the red stone house on the left in front of the

❻ Circo di Massenzio
❼ Grave of Romulus

❽ Mausoleo di Cecilia
Metella

Mass in the Domitilla Catacombs on the Via Appia Antica

Villa Quintili on the Via Appia Antica was built in around 150 CE

9 Trattoria "Qui nun se more mai"

10 Via C. Metella kiosk

Cecilia Metella mausoleum. If you've not worked up an appetite by now, keep the **9** Trattoria "Qui nun se more mai" *(Tue–Sat noon–11pm, Sun noon–3pm | Via Appia Antica 198 | €–€€)*, in mind for your return journey. In English, its name means "Here you'll never die" and they serve authentic, homely Roman fare. But maybe a snack from the **10** Via C. Metella kiosk, is enough to keep you going. You can sit on the wooden benches to catch your breath and enjoy a *panini* filled with ham and cheese and a choice of coffee or cold drinks.

ROMAN VS RING ROAD

Now comes the most attractive part of the route, through pines and cypresses. You pass lots of graves – in ancient times burials within the city walls were prohibited – covered with ivy, poppies and daisies. The old Roman paving has also been excavated here.

INSIDER TIP
Paradise starts now

Caesar's carriages had such good suspension – almost definitely better that your bicycle's saddle – that the emperor could travel long distances on this ancient surface in comfort. Another attraction is the nymphaeum of the ⑪ Villa Quintili, *after about Km8*. The gate is usually locked but it is still worth seeing from outside. *After about Km10*, you'll notice on your left the arches of the ⑫ Aquedotto dei Quintili. Your tour ends here where the old Roman road meets the *Raccordo Anulare*, the ring road (underpass available). On the return stretch, you'll be treated to romantic views of decorated graves, ruins and the Roman *campagna*, which the great German poet Goethe enjoyed so much.

⑪ Villa Quintili

⑫ Aquedotto dei Quintili

⑤ TAKE THE TRAIN TO THE MED: OSTIA & OSTIA ANTICA

- ➤ Ancient advertising featuring nymphs and sea monsters
- ➤ Ostia Antica, protected by the hand of Neptune, God of the Sea
- ➤ Swimming and clubbing

📍 Piazzale Ostiense

🏁 Lido di Castel Fusano

➡ 35km

🚌 1 day (2 hrs total travel/walking time)

ℹ Ostia gets very busy on summer weekends when it becomes a beach and clubbing haven for young Romans.

POLICE, FIRE & THE TAVERNE DES FORTUNATO

Suburban trains to Ostia and Ostia Antica leave from ① Piazzale Ostiense (🚋 *1.50 euros | Metro B Piramide*). The journey to the *Ostia Antica* takes around 25 minutes. *An overpass gets you safely over the Via del Mare after which it is only around 400m to the entrance to the ruined city of* ② Ostia Antica. Wander along the main street, Decumanus Maximus, until you get to

① Piazzale Ostiense

22 km

② Ostia Antica

7.7 km

Baths of Neptune (best view of the mosaics is from the first floor). Then continue via the Caserma dei Vigili, (the police and fire stations) until you get to the Bar of Fortunatus where a 2,000-year-old mosaic tells drinkers, "Drink wine from the vessel because you are thirsty". After the well-preserved Teatro Romano (open for performances in summer) you will reach the Piazzale delle Corporazioni, where you can see how sponsoring worked in the Roman period. Nymphs, sea monsters, dolphins and galleys act as advertising hoardings for the traders who financed the theatre more than 2,000 years ago. Unlike Pompeii or the Roman Forum, you will probably be able to tour Ostia Antica in relative seclusion.

> **INSIDER TIP**
> Advertising the Roman way

PRICEY PARASOLS & PUBLIC BEACHES

Return to *Stazione Ostia Antica* and take the train to the *Stazione Castel Fusan* in ❸ Lido di Ostia. The popular fish restaurant ❹ La Vecchia Pineta *(Piazzale dell' Aquilone 4 | tel. 06 56 47 02 82 | lavecchiapineta.com | €€–€€€)* on the promenade reels its guests in with delicious dishes served on a terrace right on the water's

❸ Lido di Ostia

350 m

❹ La Vecchia Pineta

edge. Access to the sea is strictly controlled by the private beach mafia. Romans love expensive beach clubs like the legendary Kursaal *(Lungomare Lutazia Catulo 36 | kursaalvillage.com)* and Stabilimento Balneare Venezia *(Lungomare Amerigo Vespucci 8–12 | stabilimentoilvenezia.com)*. A parasol and two loungers will set you back around 30 euros (with swimming pool included) … You could just get a drink instead and *take a shuttle bus (no. 7) further south from Cristoforo Colombo station on the promenade.* Stay on the bus until you see a series of dunes looming up ahead of you. The beaches here, at ❺ Lido di Castel Fusano, are free and the water is cleaner too. At Km7.8 there are a couple of cool, improvised beach bars..

4.8km

❺ Lido di Castel Fusano

Mosaic flooring in Ostia Antica

GOOD TO KNOW

HOLIDAY BASICS

ARRIVAL

GETTING THERE BY PLANE

Flights to Rome from London take around 2.5 hours (a little longer from other UK airports and Ireland). This sounds quick, but getting from the airport into central Rome adds a good chunk of time. Rome has two airports. The main one is *Aeroporto Leonardo da Vinci* in Fiumicino, around 32km outside Rome, and is used by the larger, more expensive airlines like BA as well as by Easyjet.

Adapter Type L

This old type of plug is gradually being replaced with standard EU ones (and most EU adapters should work).

INSIDER TIP
And then let's go

The Leonardo Express airport rail service is cheaper and quicker than taking a taxi to the centre *(14 euros, tickets from the ticket machines in front of the platform in the airport train station | from the airport 6.23am-11.23pm every 30 mins; from Stazione Termini*

(platform 25) 5.35am-10.35pm every 30 mins).

It's even cheaper to take a *Terravision* bus (stops at Terminal 3). A ticket costs 6 euros and it takes 20 minutes to get to Stazione Termini *(Via Marsala 29, platform 1).* Book in advance online.

Rome's second airport, *Ciampino*, is actually a bit closer to the city but has worse transport connections. Other budget carriers such as Ryanair land here. A taxi to the city centre (around 18km) will cost about 35 euros. There

Colonnades in the Piazza San Pietro

are *Terravision* buses every hour costing 6 euros to Stazione Termini. The journey takes about 40 minutes and should also be booked in advance.

GETTING THERE BY CAR

If you really want to spend several days with lorry drivers from across Europe, driving to Rome is an option. There are expensive tolls (in France and Italy), high fuel prices and of course lots of traffic (especially around the Po Valley). However, you will be treated to bella Italia's beautiful landscape, many sights just off the motorway and service stations that feel like department stores. The food is often genuinely good and the toilets are clean.

For the final stretch, leave the *Autostrada del Sole* and take the *Grande Raccordo Anulare (G.R.A)*, Rome's ring road. Keep following signs to *Roma centro* or you'll land up in a suburb.

SUSTAINABLE TRAVEL

If you want to keep your carbon footprint in check while on holiday you can offset your CO_2 emissions (*myclimate.org*). There are also tools to help you plan lower carbon journeys (*routerank.com*). And while you're away, be sensitive to the natural world. To find out more about sustainable travel go to *sustainabletravel.org*.

GETTING THERE BY TRAIN

Most trains from the north terminate at *Stazione Termini* or at the new *Stazione Tiburtina*, in the north. Italy has extremely fast trains nowadays. The *Freccia Rossa* (the red arrow), covers the distance between Milan and Rome in just three hours and gets you to Naples in a shade over an hour. Info at: *tel. 89 20 21 | ferroviedellostato.it |*

trenitalia.com. Bookings can be made online, through travel agents and at major stations.

CLIMATE AND WHEN TO GO

Rome's mild Mediterranean climate and the prospect of 300 days of sun make it an attractive place to visit. The best months to go are March, April and May when the blossom is out and the city is in full pink bloom. Note: Half of Christendom comes to the Vatican at Easter, and much of the other half is at the Colosseum so hotel rooms are hard to come by. It gets very hot from July onwards and the city empties out in August because sightseeing in 36°C feels more like marine survival training than a holiday. Lots of restaurants and shops close for the month. The best thing to do in summer is to enjoy the warm evenings of the *estate romana* by going to outdoor concerts and cinemas and to make the most out of cheap hotel prices.

Mid-September to late October is another great time to visit with pleasantly warm days. It rains more in November and December but generally not for very long. There is very rarely snow in Rome. Pictures of snowball fights on St. Peter's Square or angels covered in white may be widespread but they don't represent reality. January and February can get more unpleasant, when the bitingly cold *Tramontana* blows down from the mountains; but there will still be days you can drink a cappuccino outside. However, lots of shops are shut in January.

GETTING AROUND

BIKES & MOPEDS

Bike and moped hire is becoming increasingly popular, e.g. *Roma rent a bike (▥ D9) (Via di San Paolo alla Regola 33/at Campo de' Fiori | tel. 06 88 92 23 65 | www.romarentbike. com); Roma rent a Scooter (▥ B7) (Via del Paradiso 42/near the Vatican Museum | tel. 0 66 87 72 39| www. romarentscooter.com); Rome by Vespa (▥ J7) (Via dei Mille 8, near Stazione Termine | tel. 06 42 22 78 | romeby vespa.com);* and *Bici e baci (▥ G-H7) (Via del Viminale 5 | www.bicibaci.com)* or *Via Cavour 302 (▥ F-G9).* Bici e Baci also hire Vespas and organize cycle tours, e.g. along the Via Appia Antica.

If you would like to hire an electric bike, then head for *Ecovia Bici Eletriche (▥ G9) (Via Cardello 32 | tel. 06 45 50 89 23 | www.ecovia.it).* Segways can be hired at various stations around Rome for about 15 euros an hour, for example, at the entrance to the large *Villa Borghese Park (▥ F6).* A three-hour classic tour of Rome costs about 80 euros *(www. romebysegway.com).*

DRIVING

Italy's traffic regulations have become stricter and fines are steep. Seat belts must be worn, and moped riders must wear a helmet. The speed limit on three-lane motorways is 130kmh (110kmh if it is raining). Outside built-up areas cars must drive with their lights on. Remember to have a fluorescent jacket in case of a breakdown when leaving the car outside built-up areas – the fine for not having one is 137 euros. When taking a rental car, check it has a vest. Drink-driving regulations are strict too: the maximum blood alcohol content is 0.5g per litre.

Touring Club Italiano provides information for drivers including up-to-date road conditions. *Mon–Sat 10am–7pm | Piazza Santi Apostoli 22 | tel. 06 36 00 52 81 | touringclub.it | bus 280 | ▥ F8*

PUBLIC TRANSPORT

There are relatively few trams, buses and Metro trains running, especially at the weekend. Up-to-date information is available at *atac.roma.it*.

A *BIT* ticket for bus or Metro costs 1.50 euros *(single trip, valid for 100 mins)*; a day ticket costs 7 euros (two days 12.50 euros, three days 18 euros). Buy them from a transport authority (ATAC) office, e.g. in front of *Stazione Termini (▥ H8)*, *Piazza San Silvestro (▥ E7)* or at one of the many tobacconists and kiosks with the black, red and yellow ATAC sign. The tickets have to be stamped in the bus, Metro or tram.

Rome has three Metro lines. *Linea A*: Battistini to Anagnina (southeastern suburb, towards Castelli Romani); *Linea B*: Rebibbia to EUR-Laurentina; and *Linea B1*: Piazza Bologna to Conca d'Oro. *Linea C* is new and goes from Montecompatri/Pantano to San Giovanni in the Lateran. They run *Sun–Thu*

5.30am–11.30pm, Fri/Sat 5.30–1.30am. There are ticket machines at station entrances.

BUS TO VIA APPIA

The best route is to take bus 218 from Piazza di Porta San Giovanni in Laterano *(▥ J10)* (Metro A San Giovanni) to Via Appia Antica. Bus 118 also travels from Piazzale Ostiense *(▥ F13)* (Metro B Piramide). On Sundays, it is advisable to take a taxi as only a handful of buses will be running.

TAXI

Taxis are cheaper than black cabs in the UK and the taximeters are calibrated properly and checked. The basic price is 3 euros. Supplements: night rate from 10pm 6.50 euros; Sundays and holidays 4.50 euros. The first 10km cost 1.10 euros, from then on 1.30–1.60 euros. The first piece of luggage is free, 1 euro for every further piece. Don't be taken in by scams! They may seem friendly but you'll pay for it. Only use official white taxis at taxi ranks or the MyTaxi app. *Minicabs: tel. 06 49 94, 06 66 45 and 06 35 70.*

EMERGENCIES

EMERGENCY NUMBERS

Police (Carabinieri): *tel. 112, 113*
Fire brigade: *tel. 115*
Ambulance: *tel. 118*
ACI breakdown service: *tel. 116*

HEALTH

24-hour pharmacies: *Farmacia Internazionale (□□ H8) Piazza dei Cinquecento 51 | Stazione Termini* and *(□□ C6) Via Cola di Rienzo 213.*

First aid *(pronto soccorso)* is free of charge in all hospitals. For citizens of the EU, the European insurance card EHIC entitles you to treatment (sometimes with additional fees). Visitors from non-EU countries should take out private insurance.

Children's hospital: *Ospedale dei Bambin Gesú (□□ B8) Piazza S. Onofrio | tel. 0 66 85 91*

CONSULATES & EMBASSIES
BRITISH EMBASSY
Via XX Settembre 80a | 00187 Roma RM / tel. 06 42 20 00 01 | ukinitaly.fco. gov.uk

U.S. EMBASSY ROME
Via Vittorio Veneto 121 | 00187 Rome | tel. 06 46741 | it.usembassy.gov

IRISH EMBASSY ROME
Villa Spada al Gianicolo | Via Giacomo Medici 1 | 00153 Rome | tel. 06 585 2381 | dfa.ie/irish-embassy/italy

CANADIAN EMBASSY ROME
Via Salaria, 243 | 00198 Roma | tel. 06 85 44 41 | canadainternational.gc.ca/ italy-italie

LOST & FOUND
The city's lost property office *(Ufficio degli Oggetti Rinvenuti)* is in the Circonvallazione Ostiense 191 *(□□ F14) (Mon–Fri 8.30am–1pm, Thu 8.30am–5pm | tel. 06 67 69 32 14*

| www.oggettismarriti@comune.roma. it | Metro B Garbatella).

THEFT
If you are a victim of theft, notify the nearest police or *carabinieri* station or the *questura* (police administration). Interpreters are available to record the details. *Via San Vitale 1 | tel. 0 64 68 61 | Metro A Repubblica | bus 60, 64, 70, 7 | □□ G8*

ESSENTIALS

BANK HOLIDAYS

1 Jan	New Year's Day
6 Jan	Epiphany
March/April	Easter Sunday/Monday
25 April	Liberation from Fascism
1 May	Labour Day
2 June	Festival of the Republic
29 June	St Peter and St Paul's Day
15 Aug	Assumption Day
1 Nov	All Souls' Day
8 Dec	Immaculate Conception
25/26 Dec	Christmas

BANKS
All banks *(banca)* and savings banks *(cassa di risparmio)* have cashpoints (ATMs) open 24 hours a day. For other banking services they are usually open Mon–Fri 8.30am–3/4pm.

CUSTOMS
Unlimited goods for personal use can be imported and exported without paying duties within the EU. If coming from outside the EU, be careful to check your allowances. Fines can be extreme.

HOW MUCH DOES IT COST?

Espresso	0.90 euro at the counter
Ice cream	3 euros for a large portion
Panino	4–6 euros for a large sandwich
T-Shirt	10 euros for a souvenir T-shirt
Bus ticket	1.50 euros for a single
Club entry	from 20 euros per person

INTERNET & WIFI

Most hotels have WiFi – *rete senza fili* in Italian – but occasionally they still charge for it. Thanks to *www.digitroma.com* (online registration necessary) you can surf free of charge for up to four hours a day at many of the nicest city squares and in many parks. Good cafés with WiFi include: *The Library (Vicolo della Cancelleria 7 | thelibrary.it); Mecanismo Bistrot (Piazza Trilussa 34);* and *Pimm's Good Bar (Via di San Dorotea 8–9).*

PILGRIMS & PAPAL AUDIENCES

Christians of all denominations should be able to find organisations to help them arrange a pilgrimage to Rome by looking online or by speaking to their local vicar or priest.

When the Pope is in Rome, he holds a general audience on St Peter's Square on Wednesdays at 10.30am and says the Angelus prayer from the window of the Vatican Palace on Sundays at noon *(www.vatican.va).* Tickets for papal audiences can be acquired online *(vatican.va, under "Infos")* or from the Swiss Guard at the "Bronze Door" (on the day before you want to go). You don't need a ticket if you are happy to stand in St. Peter's Square, but you will have to go through security.

PHONE & MOBILE PHONE

The Italian for mobile is *cellulare* or *telefonino*. There is good coverage across the city. Most of the time you will be picked up the provider *TIM (Telecom Italiana Mobile).* To call home, make sure you include the international country code (0044 for the UK, 00353 for Ireland, 001 for USA and Canada). To call Italian numbers you need to make sure you use their country code, 0039.

All phone numbers in Rome start with 06 – whether you make a call from within the city, from somewhere else in Italy or from abroad. Only Italian mobile phones don't start with a "0".

TABACCHI SHOPS

The Romans love their distinctive *tabacchi* shops with the white "T" on a black background. Once they sold tobacco products, salt and official documents but today you are more likely to get newspapers, bus tickets and stamps (among many other things). Warning: some shopkeepers will sing the praises of different postal services like *friendpost (friendpost.it)* and *GPS (globepostalservice.com),* which are meant to be more reliable and are definitely more expensive. They have nothing to with the Italian postal

service which may be very, very slow but is reliable enough that things reach their destination. On the subject of stamps: *Poste Vaticane* on St Peter's Square does not only do the best stamps but is also an extremely reliable service.

INSIDER TIP
Heavenly postal service

TIPPING

Tipping is common in Italy even if some bloggers claim it is not. Some people in service jobs depend on tips. Here are some suggestions for the right amount: give waiters 5–10 per cent depending on how satisfied you were; hotel cleaners 1–2 euros/day or 4–5 euros/week; porters 1–2 euros. Taxi drivers *expect* nothing.

TOURIST INFORMATION: INFO LINE AND INFO PAVILIONS

If you call the info line (06 06 08) and press "5" you will be able to get tourist information in both Italian and English. Call them to find out about bus routes, concerts, events, etc (also available online at *060608.it/en*).

There are tourist information pavilions *(9.30am–7pm)* at many of the tourist hotspots including Castel Sant'Angelo *(Piazza Pia)* *(*[ ]*C7)*; Corso *(Via Minghetti)* *(*[ ]*E8)*; Via dei Fori Imperiali *(opposite the Roman Forum* *(*[ ]*F9)*; Stazione Termini *(by platform 24, entrance also from Via Giolitti 34)* *(*[ ]*J8)*; Piazza Cinque Lune *(near Piazza Navona)* *(*[ ]*D8)*; and Via Nazionale *(Palazzo Esposizioni)*. *(*[ ]*G8)*

TOURS

For information about the *Roma Pass* *(romapass.it)*, see p. 9. Personal guided tours or double-decker bus tours are a great way to see Rome's attractions.

LINEA 110 – RED DOUBLE-DECKER

Hop-on, hop-off. *Daily 8.30am–7pm every 20 mins | Piazza Cinquecento (Stazione Termini)* *(*[ ]*H8)* *| 20 euros/ 24 hrs or 25 euros/48 hrs*

ROMA CRISTIANA – PILGRIM LINES

The hop-on, hop-off double-decker

buses run by the Roman pilgrim organisation take you to the seven pilgrimage churches and other Roman Catholic sights. *Daily 9.30am–6pm | Via della Conciliazione (St Peter's Square) (▦ B7) | 20 euros/24 hrs or 23 euros/48 hrs | operaromanapellegrinaggi.org*

ROME OPEN TOUR – PINK DOUBLE-DECKER

You're probably familiar with the hop-on, hop-off principle: you pay once and you can hop on and off anytime. *Daily departures 9am–7pm every 20 mins, Nov–mid-March 9am–5pm | Piazza Cinquecento (Stazione Termini) (▦ H8) | 22 euros/24 hrs or 28 euros/48 hrs | romeopentour.it*

THROUGH ETERNITY TOURS

Sophisticated personal city tours by art historians and archaeologists to Rome's underworld and on the trail of Caravaggio. *Tel. 06 700 93 39 | www. througheternity.com*

ROMAMIRABILIA

City tours with art historians, as well as cookery classes, gourmet or Vespa tours and incentive-building workshops for corporate groups. *Tel. 06 45 49 73 72 | www.romamirabilia. com*

WALKS INSIDE ROME

An agency with loads of experience and plenty of options including 👥 kids and families tours around Rome's historical sights. *Tel. 06 66 24 626 | walksinsiderome.com*

WEATHER

High season
Low season

	JAN	FEB	MARCH	APRIL	MAY	JUNE	JULY	AUG	SEPT	OCT	NOV	DEC
Daytime temperatures in °C	11°	13°	16°	19°	23°	28°	31°	31°	27°	21°	16°	12°
Night time temperatures in °C	4°	5°	7°	10°	13°	17°	20°	20°	17°	13°	9°	5°
☀️	4	4	5	7	8	10	11	10	7	6	5	4
🌧️	8	9	8	8	7	4	2	2	5	8	10	10
≈	14°	13°	13°	14°	17°	21°	23°	24°	23°	20°	18°	15°

☀️ Sunshine hours/day　　🌧️ Rainy days/month　　≈ Sea temperatures in °C

USEFUL WORDS & PHRASES

SMALLTALK

An accent in Italian means the last syllable must be emphasised. Otherwise we have put dots below the stressed syllable.

Yes/no/maybe	sì/no/forse
Please/thank you	per favore/grazie
Excuse me (formal/informal)	Scusa!/Scusi!
Sorry, I didn't catch that	Come dice?/Prego?
Good morning/afternoon/evening/night	Buon giorno!/Buon giorno!/Buona sera!/Buona notte!
Hello/bye/goodbye	Ciao!/Ciao!/Arrivederci!
My name is …	Mi chiamo …
What's your name (formal/informal)	Come si chiama?/Come ti chiami?
I would like …/Do you have …	Vorrei …/Avete …?
I (don't) like this	(Non) mi piace.
Good/bad	buono/cattivo

SYMBOLS

EATING & DRINKING

The menu, please	Il menù, per favore.
Bottle/carafe/glass	bottiglia/caraffa/bicchiere
Knife/fork/spoon	coltello/forchetta/cucchiaio
Salt	sale/pepe/zucchero
Vinegar/oil/ milk/cream/lemon	aceto/olio/latte/panna/limone
with/without ice/gas (in water)	con/senza ghiaccio/gas
Cold/over-seasoned/undercooked	freddo/troppo salato/non cotto
Vegetarian/allergy	vegetariano/vegetariana/allergia
Could I get the bill please?	Vorrei pagare, per favore.
Bill/receipt/tip	conto/ricevuta/mancia
Cash/credit card	in contanti/carta di credito

MISCELLANEOUS

Where is…?	Dove posso trovare …?
Left/right/straight on	sinistra/destra/dritto
What time is it?	Che ora è? Che ore sono?
It is three o'clock/It is half past three	Sono le tre./Sono le tre e mezza.
Today/tomorrow/yesterday	oggi/domani/ieri
How much does … cost?	Quanto costa …?
Too much/little/everything/nothing	troppo/molto/poco/tutto/niente
Expensive/cheap/price	caro/economico/prezzo
Where can I get on the internet/WIFI?	Dove trovo un accesso internet/ wi-fi?
Open/closed	aperto/chiuso
Broken/doesn't work	guasto/non funziona
breakdown/garage	guasto/officina
Timetable/ticket	orario/biglietto
Train/track/platform	treno/binario/banchina
Help!/Caution!/Look out!	Aiuto!/Attenzione!/Prudenza!
Ban/banned/danger/dangerous	divieto/vietato/pericolo/ pericoloso
Pharmacy	farmacia
Fever/pain	febbre/dolori
0/1/2/3/4/5/6/7/8/9/10/ 100/1000	zero/uno/due/tre/quattro/cinque / sei/sette/otto/nove/dieci/cento/ mille

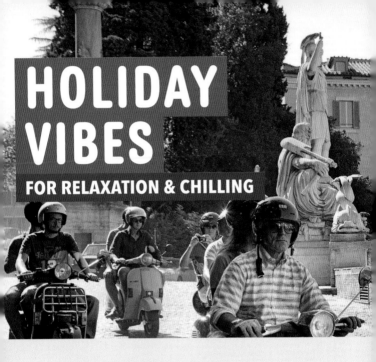

HOLIDAY VIBES
FOR RELAXATION & CHILLING

FOR BOOKWORMS & FILM BUFFS

📖 IMPERIUM

A sensitve but hugely ambitious young lawyer enters the most powerful political arena in the world. Washington? No – Rome! Robert Harris's gripping historical thriller is set in Ancient Rome, his ambitious young lawyer is none other than Marcus Tullius Cicero. History at its very coolest (2006).

🎥 LA GRANDE BELLEZZA

Paolo Sorrentino won an Oscar and a Golden Globe for this 2014 dazzling, decadent portrait of Rome. The hero is Jep Gambardella who spends his time mingling with the *crème de la crème* of Roman society. On his 65th birthday he falls into an existential crisis. The cinematography is quite beautiful.

📖 SUBURRA

A sizzling thriller set in Rome and which was turned into a Netflix series in 2017. Investigative journalist Carlo Bonini and Giancarlo de Cataldo may have invented "Samurai", the eccentric Mafia boss, but their depictions of Rome as a den of corruption and of the authorities infiltrated by the Mafia are all too real, especially in the city's suburbs.

PLAYLIST

0:58

ǁ EROS RAMAZOTTI – PIÙ BELLA COSA
This song – by one of Rome's favourite sons – nearly brought the house down at the Stadio Olimpico.

▶ CARL BRAVE & FRANCO 126 – SEMPRE IN 2
This rap anthem by a popular duo was in the Italian charts for 38 weeks. Its most poetic lyrics: "I'd like to rob the Trevi Fountain's wishes."

Your holiday soundtrack can be found on **Spotify** under **MARCO POLO** Rome

▶ PAVAROTTI, CARRERAS, DOMINGO – O SOLE MIO
The iconic three tenors' performance in the Baths of Caracalla.

▶ ANTONELLO VENDITTI – ROMA ROMA ROMA
AS Roma's anthem, sung before every game.

▶ ANDREA BOCELLI – OMAGGIO A ROMA
Andrea Bocelli's love song to the eternal city. Watch the YouTube video with the sights of Rome.

Or scan this code with the Spotify app

ONLINE

TIMEOUT.COM/ROME
The best place to find out about events and comprehensive film and theatre listings.

ANAMERICANINROME.COM
Natalie has lived in Rome since 2010 and regularly updates her blog with the latest hot tips for great places to eat and things to do in her adopted home.

DISCOTECHEAROMA.IT
The one-stop shop for clubbing info (also includes gigs and jazz concerts).

ROMEING.IT
An online magazine largely run by expats with lots of information for tourists and interesting articles on Rome past and present.

KATIEPARLA.COM/BLOG
Originally from New Jersey, Katie Parla has been living in Rome for more than a decade. Like her British counterpart Rachel Roddy, she has been able to show that foreigners can do interesting things with Italian food. Parla also offers great fun food tours and even has her own app.

TRAVEL PURSUIT

THE MARCO POLO HOLIDAY QUIZ

Do you know what makes Rome tick? Test your knowledge of the idiosyncracies and eccentricities of the city and its people. You'll find the answers at the foot of the page, with more detailed explanations on pages 20–25.

❶ What is the most free-flowing source of money here?
a) Banca di Roma Student Loans
b) EU Subsidies
c) The Trevi Fountain

❷ What souvenir did Roman generals bring back from Egypt?
a) Cleopatra
b) Obelisks
c) The Sphinx

❸ Who is the most important person in the lives of most Italians?
a) Football legend Francesco Totti
b) A good tax advisor
c) Their mamma

❹ Which is the most popular wedding venue for Roman couples?
a) The Campidoglio
b) Castel Sant'Angelo
c) The catacombs

Campidoglio

❺ Who has bought recycled fashion from the Fendi heiress, Ilaria?
a) Mother Theresa
b) Michelle Obama
c) Kim Kardashian

❻ What does *la dolce vita* mean?
a) A sweet treat
b) The good life (according to Federico Fellini)
c) The cutest dog

❼ How does the Pope most like to travel?
a) In an old Ford
b) On a consecrated Harley-Davidson
c) In a carriage

❽ What is Spanish about the Spanish Steps?
a) Paella is made on them on hot Sundays
b) Most of the tourists sitting on them are Spanish
c) The Spanish embassy was once nearby

❾ Why did a shoe company renovate the Colosseum?
a) To advertise their Roman sandal range
b) Because you can't walk around the Colosseum barefoot
c) Because the city of Rome is broke

INDEX

WE WANT TO HEAR FROM YOU!

Did you have a great holiday? Is there something on your mind? Whatever it is, let us know! Whether you want to praise the guide, alert us to errors or give us a personal tip – MARCO POLO would be pleased to hear from you. Please contact us by email:

We do everything we can to provide the very latest information for your trip. Nevertheless, despite all of our authors' thorough research, errors can creep in. MARCO POLO does not accept any liability for this.

e-mail: sales@heartwoodpublishing.co.uk

PICTURE CREDITS
Cover photo: San Pietro (Huber-images: S. Kremer)
Photos: DuMont Bildarchiv (75, F. Heuer (Front flap, outside, front flap inside, 1, 115, 120/121, 158/159), Zoltan Nagy (63, 76/77, 143); R. Freyer (93, 148/149); huber-images: Albanese (54), Bernhart (24); Huber-images: P. Canali (2/3); huber-images: M. Carassale (72/73), C. Cassaro (126/127), G. Croppi (83), Hallberg (59), S. Kremer (6/7, 26/27, 46/47, 65, 68); Huber-images: S. Kremer (132); huber-images: J. Lawrence (17), M. Mastorillo (78/79, 98), Zoltan Nagy (71), A. Piai (31), Rellini (52/53); Huber-images: M. Rellini (4); huber-images: J. Ritterbach (41), N. Russo (36), A. Saffo (160/161), S. Scatà (86), A. Serrano (8, 38/39, 50), A. Facilongo (112), F. Heuer (12/13), G. Kloetzer (137), E. Paoni (108/109), D. Schmid (94/95), W. Stahr (56), Zuder (101); Laif/Contrasto: M. Lombezzi (104); Laif/Contrasto/A3: A. Casasoli (122/123); Laif/ hemis.fr: F. Leroy (140), R. Mattes (118/119); Laif/Le Figaro: Marmara (107); Look: Pompe (44); Lookphotos: I. Pompe (67); mauritius images: I. Bölter (14/15), Mattes (11), J. Warburton-Lee (147); mauritius images/Alamy (22, 89, 103), J. Kellerman (49), B. Kinney (42); mauritius images/Alamy/Alliance (10); mauritius images/Alamy/tilialucida (144); Shutterstock: Rafael Martos Martins (25), Viacheslav Lopatin (75), Nicop46 (154); mauritius images/Imagebroker (34); mauritius images/imagebroker: Handl (9); mauritius images/Imagebroker: M. Jung (32); mauritius images/United Archives (21); H. Pabel (163); Schapowalow: G. Croppi (124/125)

5th Edition – fully revised and updated 2022
Worldwide Distribution: Heartwood Publishing Ltd, Bath, United Kingdom
www.heartwoodpublishing.co.uk

© MAIRDUMONT GmbH & Co. KG, Ostfildern
Author: Swantje Strieder
Editor: Marlis v. Hessert-Fraatz
Picture editor: Gabriele Forst
Cartography: © MAIRDUMONT, Ostfildern (pp. 33, 128–129, 131, 135, 139, 142, 146, inner flap, outer flap, pull-out map); © MAIRDUMONT, Ostfildern, using data from OpenStreetMap, Licence CC-BY-SA 2.0 (pp. 28–29, 35, 45, 55, 61, 69, 74, 80–81, 96–97, 110–111).
Cover, wallet and pull-out map design: bilekjaeger_Kreativagentur with Zukunftswerkstatt, Stuttgart
Page design: Langenstein Communication GmbH, Ludwigsburg

Heartwood Publishing credits:
Translated from the German by John Owen, John Sykes, Susan Jones and Suzanne Kirkbright
Editors: Felicity Laughton, Kate Michell, Sophie Blacksell Jones
Prepress: Summerlane Books, Bath
Printed in India

MARCO POLO AUTHOR
SWANTJE STRIEDER

As a child Swantje threw some coins into the Trevi Fountain and made a wish … which came true when she returned to the city as a foreign correspondent. She had to learn quickly that *bambini* only eat pasta and never, ever potatoes! She loves writing about life in Rome, from the café where she gets her favourite espresso to the vegetable seller at the market where she buys her weekly supplies – but she also loves the city's culture, both contemporary and ancient.

DOS & DON'TS

HOW TO AVOID SLIP-UPS & BLUNDERS

DO RESPECT THE ROMANS' HOME
Hooligans have been known to smash up sculptures, while revellers often urinate on the Spanish Steps. City centre residents are (unsurprisingly) not keen on this behaviour – please respect their home!

DO TAKE CARE ON ZEBRA CROSSINGS
Do what the Romans do: make eye contact with drivers and then confidently step into the road. It's best to cross busy roads in the slipstream of Romans who know the rules and conventions of the traffic here.

DON'T PAY TOO MUCH NOTICE TO OPENING HOURS
Listings will give you a good idea of when restaurants and shops are open. However, it's entirely possible that you will rock up at a trattoria and find its shutters down. It's just the way things are done here – if the owner goes on holiday or out for the evening, they just spontaneously shut up shop.

DON'T FLASH THE CASH
Watch out for pickpockets on public transport. Avoid carrying large amounts of money with you and leave your passports and jewellery in the hotel safe. Oh, and don't stand stock still on the bus.

DO DRINK FROM FOUNTAINS
Drinking water flows from the *fontanelle*, the small fountains in the historic centre, and it is free. At the mobile stands next to major tourist attractions, prices are exorbitant: a small bottle of mineral water or Coca-Cola costs 3-4 euros!